"I looked out of the window of the airplane, and I looked down at the Pacific Ocean, and I remember saying to myself, is this all one big dream? It was only a couple of years ago that I couldn't even walk right, much less run. Now here I am on this big charter jet going off to another country as one of the fastest women in the whole world . . ."

*For a girl still in high school, Wilma Rudolph had come a long, hard way.*

This is her story, as she lived it, as she felt it, as only she could tell it. It says a lot about what it takes to become a great athlete. It says even more about what it feels like and means to become a human being who is an inspiration to others.

# *WILMA*

# SIGNET Books of Interest

# WILMA

by
## Wilma Rudolph

Martin Ralbovsky,
Editorial Associate

A SIGNET BOOK
NEW AMERICAN LIBRARY
TIMES MIRROR

Copyright © 1977 by Bud Greenspan

 SIGNET TRADEMARK REG. U.S. PAT. OFF. AND FOREIGN COUNTRIES
REGISTERED TRADEMARK—MARCA REGISTRADA
HECHO EN CHICAGO, U.S.A.

SIGNET, SIGNET CLASSICS, MENTOR, PLUME AND MERIDIAN BOOKS
are published by The New American Library, Inc.,
1301 Avenue of the Americas, New York, New York 10019

First Signet Printing, October, 1977

1 2 3 4 5 6 7 8 9

PRINTED IN THE UNITED STATES OF AMERICA

*For the love and support of*
*Blanche Rudolph*
*Ed Temple*
*and*
*The Eldridges—Rob,*
*Yolanda, Djuana,*
*Robert and Xurry*

*Thank you.*


*Personal Thanks*
*to*
*Bud Greenspan*
*Jay Acton*
*Westly Rudolph*

# 1
## Number 20 of 22

There were twenty-two kids in my family, and nineteen of them were born before I was and two were born after. I was number 20, born in 1940, an Olympic year. (The Olympics were scheduled for Tokyo that year, but World War II canceled them.) My father worked as a porter for the railroad and he also did odd jobs around my hometown, Clarksville, Tennessee, jobs like painting people's houses and cutting firewood. My mother cleaned white people's houses to make extra money for us all, but still, when I think back to the way things were for us when I was a little girl of about four or five, my parents' combined income in a single year never amounted to more than $2,500. There was welfare back then, too, but we were never on it because my mother and my father were too proud to be taking handouts from anybody. We didn't have too much money back then, but we had everything else, especially love.

When I was four or five, just starting to become aware that I was a human being, almost all my brothers and sisters were grown up, and they had already gone and moved out of the house. All the time I grew up, there were never more than six of us in the house at one time, living in it, but the others were always coming and going, visiting or just coming home vacationing. People I never lacked for in my childhood.

I remember two things best, Christmas and the annual Clarksville county fair. Christmas was the happiest time for all of us. The brothers and sisters living out of town would come home, and they'd all have presents for us little ones. I believed in Santa Claus like no other kid believed in Santa Claus; I thought Santa Claus was God. I was five or six years old, and I would lie in bed on Christmas Eve, never falling asleep, and I would say to myself, "He is God, otherwise how could he get from place to place, all over the world, in one single night?" I worried about how he would get down people's chimneys without being burned alive. Santa Claus gave me hope; he gave me something to believe in when I was a very little girl. Then my brother Wesley went and spoiled it all one day. He said, "Wilma, I got some bad news for you. There ain't no Santa Claus." It took me a long time to get over that, especially when the next Christmas rolled by, and the next Christmas after that, and we'd all put up the little Christmas tree and decorate it with fancy balls. I used to say to myself then, "Maybe there ain't no Santa Claus, but me, I ain't taking no chances on that." I always went along with the program.

The annual county fair was held in the same spot every year, the Clarksville fairgrounds in the middle of town. We black kids used to get together and sit on the grass across from the main entrance, and we'd sit there for hours and hours, watching the white people go in and out, dressed in all of their fineries and with their fancy horses. I was four or five then, and that's when I first realized that there were a lot of white people in this world, and that they belonged to a world that was nothing at all like the world we black people lived in. We kids would sit there in the grass, this long and thick grass, and we'd actually be braiding it, pretending it was the hair on a doll's head, and changing the hair styles all day long. I remember we would all gossip. "Lookit that lady's dress, lookit that fella's fancy saddle," and then somebody said, "You notice how they do all that fussin' over them horses?" We watched closely after that and, sure enough, that's when the thought first crossed my mind, right there in the thick grass across from the fairgrounds: white people treat their horses better than they treated us black people.

So, I was five or six maybe, and my mind was working on all of this already. My mother used to go out to these people's homes, homes with all of the latest electrical gadgets, with modern plumbing and fancy bathrooms and big white pillars in the front. She would get there on Saturday mornings, and the first thing she would have to do is to serve these people with all the latest conveniences their coffee in bed. I resented that right off, my mother having to do that. We didn't have electricity in my house, and when we had to go to the

7

bathroom, we went outside, in this little shed, the outhouse. The way my mother worked, somebody should have been serving her coffee in bed on Saturday mornings. Instead, she did the serving.

I remember I was six, maybe, and I said to myself, "There's something not right about all this. White folks got all the luxury, and we black folks got the dirty work." I made up my mind right then and there. "Wilma," I said to myself, "you ain't never gonna be serving coffee to no white folks in bed on Saturday mornings."

But my mother and father were funny. I mentioned it once to my mother, when I was very young: "How come you got to do that?"

She said, "Never you mind." My mother and father were always telling us kids that we had to accept things, even though we didn't like them, that we had to accept these things because that's just the way it is. Every time one of us spoke out about something that was obviously wrong, my mother or my father would say, "Hold your tongue." A lot of black kids were raised that way down South, accepting things that weren't right, and their parents told them to accept these things because the parents thought they were protecting the children, protecting them from trouble or from pain. You accepted it, you didn't rebel against it, things would be easier for you, they figured. So they were always saying, "Hold your tongue," or "Shush up," or just plain, "Wil-MAH!"

I'll never forget, I was about six, maybe seven, and this white fellow used to come around to the black neighborhood, he'd be driving this big fancy car and always wearing a suit and a necktie. He was the insurance salesman, coming to collect his insurance payments. Even little kids knew the guy was up to no good, collecting money on black people for years and years, sometimes as much as $10,000, and when the people died, he'd pay the family two or three thousand dollars. A classic rip-off artist. But he would come around in the big car of his, wearing that suit, and the black folks would pay up, no questions asked. He had little tricks of intimidation; he would come to my house, and he would call my mother "Blanche," her first name. But he never allowed anybody to call him anything but "Mister." He would go right inside our kitchen, leave my mother standing right there in the living room, and he'd go into the kitchen and get himself a glass of water without even asking, just like he owned the house himself. No black folks even knew where he lived, much less set foot inside his house. I felt he was an intruder, a bully, and when I said something about this man, my mother gave me the usual answer—"Hold your tongue."

There was this rubber tire factory in Clarksville, and it had been in town for years. It was the big industry in the town, which had a population of between two and three thousand people, 75 percent of them white. Well, there wasn't a black kid in that town who didn't know that the rubber tire factory was against hiring black workers. As the years went by, the rubber tire factory was forced into starting to hire black workers, and when it did, the black workers got the worst jobs in the place and they were kept in these jobs no matter how good they may have been at doing something else. You grow up seeing and hearing about things like that, you get scars deep inside of you that sometimes never heal.

I remember there was this white grocery store not too far from where I lived. We would go there, and we would have to keep our mouths shut inside of the store because that was the proper ... protocol. It was protocol: white kids could giggle and act silly, black kids had to keep their mouths shut. We'd go to that white grocery store, and on the way, these white kids would call us names and taunt us, "Hey, nigger, get outa town," things like that. We had fights with them; yes, all the time. There was this big hill near the grocery store, and we black kids would go to the bottom of this hill on purpose, and we'd kinda be just waiting around for those kids to show up. We knew who they were. When they did, they started up with the nigger, nigger, nigger stuff again, and we'd go after them. These fights were nasty at times, very nasty. But we did all right in them. You know, it got to the point where we black kids used to enjoy going over to that white grocery store, and then laying low on the bottom of that hill. It was the most fun we'd have all week, the highlight.

What prompted a lot of it, in my case, I think, was the fact that at that time I didn't look like a little black girl at all. I had red, sandy hair, a light complexion, and I was skinny. My brother Wesley, the closest of my brothers to me in age and personally, he was very black. People would see us walking together, black brother and sister, and they would say, "Hey, little girl, what you doing walking with *him*?" My mother, you see, was very black, very dark. My father, on the other hand, had a very pale complexion. All of us kids seemed to be different colors. I was a little girl, and I would look at some of my brothers and sisters who were very black, and I would feel like an albino. But what all of these experiences did to me, these things I went through or saw or thought about when I was very, very young, what they did to me was leave me with a very bad feeling about white people. I thought at the time that all white people were mean and evil.

But the thing that kept a lot of us—black kids in the South then—from being bitter about life was religion. When I finally made a commitment to religion, when I was fifteen years old, it was like I had something to believe in again, almost the first thing since Santa Claus. I remember I was five, six years old, my mother used to take us to the Baptist Revival Week. They'd have this big basket rally, people would prepare boxes of food and they would spread the food out all over the place. The men would sneak off into the woods to drink whiskey, and the women all sort of looked the other way with these knowing looks. But the object of it all was to bring people together, get them involved in the church in some way.

I was about six when I first heard all of the

11

shouting and the testifying, and it was frightening to me. I always held out, never shouted or testified, not to this day. But even as a child, I understood that religion, and revival meetings and tent services, and all of the shouting and testifying, meant something to the people in the South. I understood that intuitively. Take away the churches, and the people in the South have nothing else to believe in.

Particularly the black people. Look: black people were still drinking from separate water fountains back then. Why? They couldn't get credit because the white-owned stores wouldn't give them any. Why? They couldn't even eat in the same restaurants that white people ate in. Why? All the black people in Clarksville, I remember, they all used to eat in this one place in town, Lander's Café, no place else. They weren't allowed to eat in the other restaurants in town.

But the churches didn't have restrictions. The churches said to black people, come, we've got a place for you with no questions asked. My mother was a strict Baptist; my father a little less so, but he was strict nonetheless. I think the fact that they held such strong religious beliefs affected my relationships with them, particularly my mother. She was so proud, so strong, so religious, that I didn't think I could open up to her the way I would have liked to.

I wanted to be telling her the things that little girls tell their mothers, but I couldn't. I couldn't ask about such things as sex, because sex was a taboo subject in the religion. A lot of things I wanted to know more about back then, and I should have been able to go to my mother for the answers. But I never did. I eventually found the answers on my own. My father was a very strict man around the house; he was a disciplinarian, and he ruled with an iron hand. When my father got home, everybody got quiet. Automatically. He laid down laws, laws like, "No church on Sunday mornings, no nothing else." He had a rule like that even though he rarely went to church on Sunday mornings himself. But quietly he took a lot of pride in the fact that he had twenty-two kids, and not a single one of them was ever arrested for a crime, or picked up by the police for anything, or ever went to jail. "School is the most important thing," he would tell us. He'd say, "If you get a whipping at school, the first thing you can expect when you get home is another one." He demanded that we show respect for all adults, and if we disobeyed an adult, no matter who it was, we got it from him.

He was proud of my two brothers who were in the service then; I was five years old and World War II was still going on. One brother was in the Army, the other in the Air Force. They would come home, and they would tell everybody about what they had to endure, fighting in a war overseas in the first place, and being forced to fight it in a segregated all-black unit. Both of these brothers were in segregated outfits, and they both felt that somebody up there in the Pentagon had a lot of nerve, making them fight in a war while telling them, at the same time, they weren't fit to fight it alongside white soldiers.

I remember vaguely having air-raid drills and bomb drills when I was six, hiding under the kitchen table with a sheet over my head. Right around that time, the United States dropped the atom bomb on Japan, but not too many people, black people, in Tennessee were talking about that. I didn't really know what happened until I got much older. Black people in Tennessee, they had to worry about surviving then, they didn't have time to worry about the world's problems.

I can still remember, during those years, my mother going to stores and picking up old flour sacks and bringing them home. In those days, the flour sacks had printed patterns on them, and my mother would make dresses for us out of the flour sacks. She had an old sewing machine, the kind with the foot pedal, and if you were outside playing, you could hear her working on that foot pedal all over the neighborhood. She also cooked once in a while at this white café, and she would bring extra food home for us. So we were lucky, compared to some of the black people living in the same town.

They had this place in town called the Hole in the Wall, and on Friday and Saturday nights the black men would go there and drink and listen to the blues music and forget all about their terrible existences for a couple of days. They knew that on Monday mornings they would have to get up again and do some terrible kind of work they all hated. A guy named Charlie Campbell owned that place, I remember, and he would give the men old records from the jukebox. The place helped a lot of poor black men cope with life; they never had vacations, pension plans, or trips on expense accounts. They had Friday and Saturday nights, and Sundays to sleep it all off.

Myself, I was six years old before I realized that there was something wrong with me. I was six, and I still wasn't going to school. Now, you're six, and you're supposed to be in school like the other kids. But I did have this crooked left leg, and my left foot was turned inward. I didn't hurt me physically, and the only times anybody noticed it was when I was out playing with the other kids, and some of them would start teasing me and calling me "cripple." But even that didn't bother too often because I always had brothers and sisters around, and they would stick up for me, and the teasing would stop.

But one day, this schoolteacher started showing up at my house, and then she started coming regularly three times a week and leaving work behind. I remember she left behind these books—*See Dick Run, Watch Spot Run*—and I remember looking at the pictures of these white kids having happy times all the time, and then blotting the pictures in the book right out of my head and concentrating on the words. But I knew something was wrong with me, and whatever it was was serious enough to keep me out of school. My mother had mentioned a couple of times that I had been born with polio, but I didn't know what polio was, and besides, all I had was this crooked leg anyway.

15

So I sat around the house a lot, while the other kids my age were in school. There really wasn't much to do but dream. I never saw a newspaper then, didn't know what one was. We never went to movies because we never had the money. We had a little radio, and we had one of those Victrola record players, phonographs, they called them then, with these big, black records of Billie Holliday singing the blues. So I would sit around and dream about what the rest of the world was like.

Sitting on the grass in front of the fairgrounds planted a seed in my head. It made me curious about things, especially people. I used to sit around the house, and I would tell myself, "I don't know yet what the escape is going to be, but Wilma, it's not going to be like this forever." Black people then didn't have anybody to look up to, no real heroes who were black, so most of them just blanked out the rest of the world and went about their business in very small circles. But I was always curious about what was out there; there had to be something more to life than just existing in Clarksville, Tennessee.

I knew absolutely nothing about sports then, nothing. I was six, going on seven, and I remember my brothers talking about fights, and about this guy named Joe Louis. I would say to myself, "Who in hell is Joe Louis? What does he do?" I had no idea he was the heavyweight boxing champion, and that he was black. Of course, I had no idea who the President of the United States was at the time, either.

# 2

## Scarlet Fever, Whooping Cough, and a Crooked Leg

I was a premature baby, which meant I was born before my time. My mother had me early; she fell one day, and the next thing she knew she was having me. Being a premature baby may explain why I was sick all of the time when I was growing up. I was so skinny, and I never had the strength the other kids had. I would get a common cold, and it would last for weeks, and then it would develop into something else. I was the most sickly kid in all of Clarksville. First off, a series of childhood illnesses and the fact that I never liked to eat made it difficult to grow like the other kids. My right leg was crooked and my foot twisted inward. I had double pneumonia twice. I had scarlet fever. I had whooping cough. I had the measles and the chickenpox like other kids had. I had a tonsillectomy. I had an appendectomy. In between, it seemed as if I always had a cold or a running nose or the sniffles. It was like I spent the first decade of my life being sick. It wasn't until I became a teenager that I knew what it was like to be really healthy.

During those days when I was sick all the time, my family did not have any hospitalization plans like people have today. I suffered at home. My mother used to have all of these home remedies she would make herself, and I lived on them. She was very big on hot toddys. That was a concoction of liquor, corn, sugar, and a few other things that she would cook on the stove. The toddy would get bubbling hot, and then she would make me drink it. Damned if it didn't make you feel better most of the time. Some people who were experts in making hot toddys, they used to devour them when they were perfectly healthy, just to feel better. It was the liquor, I think, that did the job, the warm liquor. Another thing my mother was big on was making me sweat. She would pile blanket on top of blanket and make me get under them and sweat. This sweating probably got rid of some of my colds, but it also was one of the reasons I was so skinny. You're not gonna be no perfect physical specimen living on hot toddys and sweating all the time.

Being sick so much kept me alone a lot. Whenever the other kids went out somewhere, I was left behind. When my mother and father went out, they'd leave me behind with one of the other kids. Being left behind had a terrible effect on me. I was so lonely, and I felt rejected. I would drift off, close my eyes, and just drift off into a sinking feeling, going down, down, down. I cried a lot. Dr. Coleman was the black doctor in town and he would come by the house every so often to check up on me; I remember him to this day as being such a beautiful man. He was so kind and nice, and he never pressured the poor black people for money. They paid him when they had it. He was a real doctor; he never sent collection agencies to people's houses with threats to pay up. He would say, "Wilma, everything is gonna turn out all right. You just fight this thing, you understand?" I tried fighting it all, but sometimes I would just get weary and gladly drift away.

After the scarlet fever and the whooping cough, I remember I started to get mad about it all. I got angry. I went through the stage of asking myself, "Wilma, what is this existence all about? Is it about being sick all the time? It can't be." So I started getting angry about things, fighting back in a new way, with a vengeance. I think I started acquiring a competitive spirit right then and there, a spirit that would make me successful in sports later on. I was mad, and I was going to beat these illnesses no matter what. No more taking what comes, no more drifting off, no more wondering. Enough was enough.

What added to this new spirit was the attitude of the kids in the neighborhood. Whenever I would come out to play, they still teased me and they would try to make me cry by saying that I was adopted, and a cripple, things like that. I used to cry, but no more. Now I said to myself, "Okay, someday I am going to show them all, someday I'll do something that will make them all take notice and put them in their places. You see, all I really wanted back then was acceptance, to be accepted by the other kids as one of them. I couldn't get that, but in a way it was good for me. It made me determined to go beyond them, to do something someday that none of them would ever do, so then they'd have to accept me. But before I did anything else, I had to get myself healthy and into the neighborhood school.

I missed kindergarten completely, and the first grade. I was finally allowed to start attending school when I was seven, and they let me in as a second-grader. The school was the Cobb Elementary School, the only all-black elementary school in Clarksville; in fact, it was more than an elementary school. It had all the grades in it, kindergarten through twelfth. It was the typical black school of its time in the South: it was inferior. The curriculum was inferior, and the black teachers did the best with what they had. The white schools had the new books and the new buildings. We got the hand-me-down books and the old redbrick buildings. All that was stressed was the basics, reading, writing, and arithmetic.

The first day I went into that school, I was terrified. I had been alone so much of my life that I was terrified of my own peer group, simply because I never spent that much time with kids my own age. I was aware, too, of the social judgments that kids made, like judging you on how much money your father made, what kind of clothes you wore, superficial things like that. It was intimidating to me, because I knew I was poor, money-wise, and I knew my clothes were made by my mother and not bought in some fancy store. School itself was one kind of pressure for me, and the kids were another kind of pressure.

I can remember in the Cobb School, the most popular kids were the principal's kids and the teacher's kids. Then came the kids who had fathers who made more money than the average black man in Clarksville. Then came the kids who came to school wearing something new every other day. That was the value system at the time. Nobody looked beyond the superficial things to see what was really there in a person. So you considered yourself lucky just to be accepted by everybody else, and not rejected as some kind of freak. Once you felt accepted, the pressure was off, and you could go about your normal business. I felt I was accepted right off as being just another kid, nothing special, just another kid, and that made me happy.

Inside, I worried a lot about losing that acceptance by doing something, or saying something, that would get the other kids down on me. So I played it safe by not doing anything, or saying much. Outwardly, I seemed happy for the first time in my life. Sometimes, I really was, especially when I would see the kids who lived far out of town, twelve or fifteen miles away, who had to get up at five o'clock in the morning to catch a bus so they could be at school at eight. I knew I didn't have it as bad as they did, and I actually felt sorry for them.

My first teacher was Mrs. Allison, and she was tremendous. I remember she also was in charge of the local Brownies, and I joined the Brownies because of her. My parents couldn't afford a Brownies' uniform, but Mrs. Allison said, "That's all right, Wilma, no big deal, instead of a uniform, you wear brown shoes or brown socks, that's good enough." She used to pick me to decorate the bulletin boards in class, and sometimes to decorate the room for little parties that we had, and I loved that.

She would read stories to us, and that was the best time in school for me that first year. I used to love to listen to her read. My mind would drift off, and I would actually be right where the story was, in the woods, or in the jungle, or wherever. And she always made us march in the local parades with the Brownie troop; she'd be there right alongside of us, marching, too. That first year of school was a big one for me; it turned my life around. I went from being a sickly kid the other kids teased to a normal person accepted by her peer group, and that was the most important thing that could have happened to me at that point in my life. I needed to belong, and I finally did.

Fourth grade was the next important year in my life. I had a teacher by the name of Mrs. Hoskins, and she was the meanest, toughest teacher in the whole school. Everybody knew her reputation for being tough, and every kid knew what he or she was getting into if they got Mrs. Hoskins. The first six weeks of that year were terrible; she was all over me for daydreaming, not paying attention, things like that. But after the shock wore off, I grew to love her. For one thing, she had no pets in class, no favorites, and she treated everybody equally. I loved that.

She actually gave me the first spanking of my life. I remember I had not done my homework, and she made me come up to the front of the room, and she swatted me a couple of times across the hand. Nobody had ever done that before to me. My mother and father never spanked me because they knew I was so sickly, and that I didn't need any more physical pain. But with Mrs. Hoskins, I was more hurt than hurt, if you know what I mean. The couple swats didn't hurt; what hurt was inside, the feeling of knowing I had done something wrong and that it was important enough to be punished for. But she made her point: she made it clear to me that she meant what she said. She never told my parents, and neither did I. I grew to love her after that, and she instilled in me that year the way to think positive. "Do it, don't daydream about it. Do it. Wilma, I want you to *do it*."

Then came the fifth grade, which was the worst year of my life. I was put in this combined fifth- and sixth-grade class; the teacher felt the fifth-graders were an imposition on him, so he ignored the fifth-graders and spent all of his time on the sixth-graders. He actually would spend weeks doing nothing else but playing checkers with this one kid in the sixth grade. He got away with it because he was good buddies with the principal. But while he was playing checkers all day, the rest of us did nothing. He used to give everybody in the class whippings across the hand for the slightest reasons. He had this big strap with a hole in the middle of it, and he'd make you come to the front of the room and hold out your hands, and then he'd smack you with the strap across them.

This led to the first act of open rebellion I ever made. I had messed up on some classwork, nothing big, and he called me to the front of the room. I knew he was going to use that strap on me so I didn't move; I sat right in my chair. Then he called me again, and I refused to budge. Finally, I did go up to the front of the room, and he said, "Hold out your hands."

I said, "No; you ain't gonna whip me for nothing. No."

"All right," he said, "maybe you'd like to go see the principal, then?"

"Yes," I said, "that will be fine." He was stunned. He finally told me to go back and take my seat, that the principal was very busy that day. But he never threatened me again with that stupid strap.

It was a big turning point for me, because I had stood up for my rights ... and won. I knew that if I went home and told my father that this teacher was beating up on kids with this strap, and that I refused to let him whip me, my father probably would have gone to the school the very next day and used the strap on him. But I didn't do that. I just contented myself with knowing that I had stood up for my rights, and that it worked for me, and it would be a lesson to carry through the rest of my life. That my older sister would learn the

24

very same lesson the same way only a couple weeks later was really ironic. But she did.

Now, in that school, the younger kids got out at two o'clock, and the older kids got out at three fifteen. I got out at two, and my sister at three fifteen. So instead of letting the younger kids walk home alone, they put us into this classroom and kept us there until three fifteen when the older kids came down and picked us up. Well, for that hour and a quarter it was like being in a concentration camp. You couldn't talk, you couldn't laugh, you couldn't leave your seat. You just sat there and waited. They put some senior in the high school in charge of the class and his job was to keep the kids in perfect order. It was terrible.

So, one day, a little before three fifteen, my sister peeks her head through the door, and says, "C'mon, Wilma, let's go home." The senior kid got mad at that, and he started scolding my sister and then he told me I couldn't go home. Then the principal came in and told my sister he was going to whip her for what she did, and my sister jumped all over him, screaming at him, and she grabbed me by the hand and the two of us ran all the way home. But the principal expelled my sister from school the next day. She was really scared, and the only way she could get back into school was if my father went to see the principal. He did, and she got back into school the day after, but whatever it was that my father said to the principal one thing happened after that: nobody ever laid a finger on any of us Rudolphs again.

All of those years of being sick left a lot of scars

on me mentally. Those years left me very insecure. I was a sensitive person to begin with, and you combine sensitivity with insecurity and you've got some case on your hands. When I was seven, eight years old, I lived in mortal fear of being disliked. I would cry if somebody just gave me a cross look. I couldn't stand to be scolded or corrected; I developed an instant dislike for whoever did such things to me. It all made me a nervous wreck.

The other side of the coin was when I would get overcome by feeling sorry for myself, I would just mope around for a couple of days and say to myself, "Nobody loves you, Wilma, you're just a sickly, ugly kid." I used to tell myself, if I could find one person in the whole world who really loved me, I'd be the happiest person on earth. Deep inside, I had an emptiness that needed filling. You're a girl, and you say to yourself, "I'm going to make sure somebody falls in love with me, and then I'll have children and I know they'll love me." I played with dolls a lot, and played house a lot, improvising, daydreaming. Then, one day I would just snap out of it and face reality again. I would say, "Wilma, first things first. You got to get rid of this brace on your leg, and you've got to get healthy."

Funny, but none of us at the time did very much thinking about the black experience in America, the very thing we were going to have to face when we grew up. The schools let us down because they never really told us what black people were going through. We'd all give the

Pledge of Allegiance to the flag every morning and never give it a second thought. We considered America our home, and we loved America, but nobody ever told us about lynchings and about slavery, and none of us ever wondered why no black person was ever the President of the United States. I guess we were just satisfied with what we had, even though it was nothing. But we didn't know it was nothing. In school, the teachers (and they were black people, too) were telling us all the time how fortunate we were, how lucky we were to have it so good. They never told us things about the black-white situation in America, but I always thought about it and wondered what those white people did besides go to the Clarksville Fair with their horses.

We had a Negro history course, even in the elementary school. But it was geared to providing us with black heroes, not telling us the facts of life. The object of it all was to give us black kids somebody to be proud of, not to tell us that we were still oppressed. The teachers used to say, "You should be proud of Booker T. Washington, because he sacrified for you." I used to say, "Gee, that's nice, how'd he know me when he's been dead all these years?" Paul Robeson I discovered myself in a library; I used to pull books all the time and read them, even though I didn't understand a lot of what was being written.

The schools down South were just like the black parents down South—they didn't tell you a lot of things, things that were the hard truths, because they felt they were protecting us. They were, in effect, protecting us by keeping us stupid, but their intentions, as they saw them, were good. But still, there's no excuse whatsoever for a black kid in Tennessee being in the sixth grade and not knowing a thing about slavery in America. God, I'm sure my great-grandparents on both sides were slaves, but to this day I'm not positively sure because my parents never told me, and even my two grandfathers never once discussed the subject with us. I'll have to trace it all back myself if I'm ever going to know, one way or the other.

So, I'm twelve years old by this time, and I'm in the sixth grade, and I'm a very confused, unhappy girl. I still didn't know a thing about sports and had never really played in any kind of a sports event. The brace was still on my leg, even though I cheated all the time and took it off when nobody was looking. The first time I ever saw actual real, live sports was on holidays when my father used to put together this baseball team, local guys, and go over to the next town and play their guys. He would take me along, and I'd be fascinated. Fourth of July, Memorial Day, weekends like that they'd play. But I still had not seen a single track meet or basketball game, and I had no idea these things existed. We didn't have a television set at home, and there was no way of knowing that in 1952, when I was twelve, the Olympic Games were being held in Helsinki, Finland. If somebody had told me that summer, "Wilma, you're going to be in the next Olympics yourself," I would have looked at him and said, "Man, you are crazy!"

# 3

## The Brace, the Treatments, the Bus Rides

The brace went on my right leg when I was five, and I lived with that thing for the next half-dozen years. It was a steel brace, and it hooked onto my leg just above the knee and went all the way down my leg and connected to my shoe. The brace was supposed to keep the leg straight all the time and prevent me from walking on the leg sideways. I used to put it on as soon as I got up in the morning, and I wasn't allowed to take it off until I went to bed at night. I wore a brown Oxford shoe with that brace, and every time I needed a new pair of shoes, it would be the same kind, brown Oxfords. It turned me into a shoe freak. When I got older, I used to splurge on shoes, open-toed shoes, patent-leather shoes, high heels, anything. Wearing those brown Oxfords all the time made me appreciate shoes more than anything else. As for the brace, it was like any other brace—it weighed a couple pounds, and it looked so terrible; it always reminded me that something was wrong with me. Psychologically, wearing that brace was devastating.

29

When I was six, I started treatments for the leg that lasted until I was ten years old. The home exercises weren't enough anymore, so my mother made arrangements for me to go to the Meharry Medical School in Nashville every week for therapy and treatments. The hospital was a black hospital, founded by two black doctors. For the first couple of years, I went there twice a week. I always took a bus, with my mother or with an aunt if my mother couldn't go with me. I'd spend around four hours in the hospital every time, and, with the bus rides back and forth, that meant the whole day was spent trying to heal up my leg. The hospital was about fifty miles from Clarksville, and the bus rides would be about an hour going and an hour coming back. But even under those circumstances, they added a dimension to my life that the other kids didn't have. I was getting out of Clarksville, I was seeing other things, even though it was the same things every time. I was traveling.

When I first went to the hospital, I remember, they would put me on tables and conduct all of these examinations. They were forever pulling, turning, twisting, lifting that leg. Then they started stringing my leg up in this thing, I think it was traction, for about an hour every visit. I would just lie there on the table, and my leg would be strung up in the air, and I would wonder, "What the hell is all this about?" My mother used to sit with me, and when she couldn't, the nurses would come in and read me stories. Then they would take the leg down and start massaging it, and then they would put it into the whirlpool. I remember that whirlpool being very, very hot, and I remember hating to put my leg in that hot water, but my mother would tell me, "Wilma, the key element here is not the water, it's the heat."

I would get home at night and sneak off into an empty room, and I would study that leg all the time, study it to see if it was getting better. There had to be some visible improvement, I would tell myself, after all of this, there just had to be. For a long time, I really didn't see an improvement, the leg was still crooked and I still had to wear the brace. I knew very little was happening, but I didn't let other people know that. So what happened was, I learned how to fake a no-limp walk. Some people, they know how to fake a limp, put one on so people think there is something wrong. Me, I learned how to fake a normal walk so that people would think there's nothing wrong. The natural feeling for me was to favor the leg, because it was pulling me off balance a little bit, but I went against the grain and forced myself to walk normally. That way, people would see me walking normally, especially my mother, and they would say to themselves, "Hey, look at Wilma walking so straight; the leg must be getting better."

I was nine and a half years old when I first took off the brace and went out in public without it. I'll never forget it. I went to church, and I walked in without the brace, and I knew right off that people were looking at me, saying to themselves, "Hey, there's Wilma, and she doesn't have the brace on her leg anymore." After church, a lot of

31

people came over, adults, and they said, "Tremendous, Wilma, you got rid of the brace, everything's gonna be real fine now." The kids, I remember, they lay back and they just watched, didn't say much, you know; it was as if they were thinking, "Okay, the brace is gone, we've got to find something else to pin on her now." I just smiled and beamed and didn't say much. But looking back on it, I'd say it was one of the most important moments of my life. From that day on, people were going to start separating me from that brace, start thinking about me differently, start saying that Wilma is a healthy kid, just like all the rest of them.

But I wasn't out of the woods yet, not by a long shot. Every night, my mother used to boil this big kettle of water on the kitchen stove, and then she'd take this hot-water bottle and fill it up and wrap it with a towel and put it on my leg. The towel kept the hot-water bottle from burning me, but the water inside was so hot I could barely stand it. She would keep saying, "It's not the water, Wilma, it's the heat." Meanwhile, I kept going back and forth to Nashville every week for those treatments. How my family paid for all of that, I will never know. But that hospital was dedicated to helping poor black people in Tennessee, and almost everybody in the place was poor. Nobody had hospitalization plans back then, and I'm sure those bills piled up. My mother may still be paying off that hospital bill today, for all I know. But I suspect that the hospital was more interested in helping people than in making money, and the doctors knew we didn't have any money and they just said, "Forget about the money for now, let's try and help this kid."

What I remember best about those years of treatments is the bus rides. Always a Greyhound bus, always the same route, and always the people who were black sat in the back. I remember the little bus station in Clarksville; it had a black ticket window, a black waiting area, a black bathroom. You were black, and you went to the bus station, you didn't even get near the white people who were making the same trip. When you got to Nashville, you might be hungry but too bad. There was this little restaurant in the Nashville bus station, and it was for whites only. You were black, you had to find someplace else to eat. When we got on the bus, my mother and I, or my aunt and I, we would automatically go to the back, and we'd sit two, three rows up from the last row on the bus. The rest of the black people would fill up around us. Every once in a while, the bus would get very crowded, like around the Christmas holidays, and if there were white people who didn't have a seat, the black people were expected to get up and give them their seats, and the black people would stand in the aisles the whole way. That was the way it was in the South back then, back in the late forties. Black people sitting in the backs of buses was a way of life, like people eating turkeys on Thanksgiving.

The bus driver, I remember, was the enforcer. If some black person made the mistake of sitting too close to the front of the bus, the driver would get up out of his seat and go over to that black person and tell the black person, "Go sit in the back, this section of the bus is reserved for whites only." The black people at the time accepted all of this without complaining. When they got to where they were going, they were always the last ones off the buses, too, and they never complained about that, either. But it affects you inside, it makes you think less of yourself, destroys your self-esteem. I was on that same bus from Clarksville to Nashville a couple times a week for four years, I don't know how many trips, and never once did I see a black person resist, or object, to sitting in the back. That just goes to show, I think, how much damage had already been done to black people in the South by that time. Not only were they being humiliated and degraded but they were actually keeping the whole thing going by resigning themselves to it all and by actually going along with it all and not fighting back or standing up for their rights.

I started using those bus trips to play out my childhood fantasies. I would kneel and look out the window, and I would see farms and barns and white picket fences, and I would make up little stories in my head and use them for the settings. I saw the seasons change on that bus route, saw the same houses in the summertime and in the winter with snow on them. I saw the same horses and cows along the way, saw them so much I thought I actually knew them. I would daydream: Someday I am going to have a big, beautiful house just like that, and my kids are going to be out front of it playing, and I'll have horses in the back and a nice, white, pretty picket fence. All my fantasies were played out on the bus ride from home to the hospital. On the way back, I would mostly sleep, because I'd be so tired out from the treatments. The only time I would wake up was to eat a sandwich my mother bought back in Nashville for me. That was one way black people back then got around the whites-only restaurants. They either brought their own food on bus trips or else they stocked up on sandwiches to go—sandwiches and candy bars and little snacks.

I prayed a lot, too. When we were very young, my mother taught us all how to pray. We all got special prayers that we learned. My mother taught us this one prayer and I'm pretty sure everybody in my family knew it backwards and forwards. It was: "Now I lay me down to sleep, I pray the Lord my soul to keep; if I should die before I wake, I pray the Lord my soul to take." As we all got older, we started incorporating other things at the tail end of the prayer, things like, "and God bless Mommy and Daddy and all the brothers and the sisters, and we pray that ..." Then we would add our own special things, and I would say, "I pray that this leg gets better and I can be healthy like everybody else." I can remember that sometimes we kids would all pray together, and once the other kids said, "and we pray that Wilma gets well so she can play with all the other boys and girls." I was really moved by that, and I loved them all very much for praying for me.

My mother and father went through a lot during those years of my illnesses and treatments. Especially my mother. But for all the work she did on my behalf, for all the pain I knew she suffered, I never once saw my mother cry. She was that strong. Even when I lost my father many years later, she didn't cry. It was her strong religious beliefs that held her together. She never once cried in front of any of us kids. She showed very little emotion of any kind in front of us, as a matter of fact. She was not one for words or feelings, but in those days, you know, a wife didn't say or do very much. The husband ran the show. When my mother and father had a discussion, it was always behind closed doors. I never once heard them discuss anything. They always felt that kids were not big enough to hear adult conversations.

My mother was more educated than my father—that means she could read and write, and my father couldn't. Still, when something needed to be read, she read it aloud to my father, and he made the decisions. Yet, in a strange way, I was closer to my father than to my mother. My father you could talk to and he would talk back. I would talk with my mother and there was always the vibration there; I knew without her even speaking, you know, what she would say. If she didn't say anything, then I knew right away the answer was no. But I loved my mother in the sense that I would go over and hug her and give her a kiss; nothing at all would be said, but we both knew there was love there.

During those years of hospital treatments, I had

one fringe benefit: I got out of doing a lot of household chores. Every kid in the family had certain chores to do around the house, but I didn't do too much of anything. I was sort of the house pet. I just moved around from one chair to another chair, and nagged and bugged everybody who was doing something. I would ask these mean little questions about what they were doing, and how they were doing it. They would always take the time to explain things to me, like "Poor Wilma, she's so hopeless, let her in on something." Then I would go to the next brother or sister, and then to the next one after that, and right on down the line, until all of the chores were finished. It was like they were doing all the work, and I was doing all the entertaining. My brothers, they did the heavy work around the house, like cutting firewood. My sisters would do things like washing the dishes. I never felt guilty about being excused from chores because of my leg; I never felt guilty because I felt I really did have a little role, and that was to keep the rest of them going. I was like a gimpy-legged cheerleader.

The houses we lived in during those years were the standard black houses of the time in the South. The first one was a very big wood-frame house. We had fireplaces all over the house and we had one stove in the kitchen, but we didn't have electricity. For light, we used kerosene lamps, or sometimes just candles. Our furniture was always covered with furniture covers, not so much to protect them, but so that the furniture would be neat and clean when somebody came over. We'd just take the covers off when we knew somebody was coming. We lived in another white-frame house in the same neighborhood later, and it was the same kind of house. It had fireplaces but no electricity. All the black people in Clarksville lived in those wooden-frame houses; the only brick houses in town were lived in by whites. Naturally, a lot of black men like my father lived in fear of fires; a spark from the fireplace, or a knocked-over kerosene lamp, and everything goes up in flames. It happened a lot, too, black families' houses burning down, sometimes killing the people inside of them.

I finally stopped the treatments at the hospital in Nashville when I was ten, but I wore the brace on and off until I was twelve. I would only wear it the last couple of years whenever the leg ached or felt uncomfortable. Then, one glorious day, my mother wrapped up the brace and sent it back to the hospital in Nashville. I was free at last.

My whole life suddenly changed just as I was ending my sixth-grade year in school. No more brace; I was healthy all over my body for the first time. I was starting to become happy all the time, playing with the other kids as a peer at last. I would be going into the seventh grade in the fall, and there was a brand-new junior-senior high school waiting for me. I felt at that point that my life was beginning at last. That summer, I went over to this playground in town, and all the kids were around, playing a game called basketball. I watched them for a while, saw how much fun they were having, studied what they were doing, and I said to myself, "Wilma, tomorrow . . . tomorrow you're going to see what it feels like to play a little basketball."

# 4

## Enter Sports

The seventh grade. That year was, as they say, one of the pivotal years of my life. The brand-new school was invigorating; it gave all of us kids something to look forward to each day. Now, to the black kids in Clarksville, school was everything. Nobody missed a day of school because nobody wanted to miss anything. Your whole social life revolved around school, and a lot of kids got involved in extra things, things that would keep them around the school after hours. They got involved because hanging around the school and doing things was a lot better than going home.

The new school in Clarksville was called the Burt High School, and it was a school that started with seventh-graders and ended with twelfth-graders. It was named after Dr. Burt, one of the leading black doctors in Tennessee. I saw him once, when he was real old, sitting in a wheelchair. But he had already done all his good works for black people, long before I was born. This new school had a girls' basketball team, and it didn't matter if you were a seventh-grader or a twelfth-grader, you were still eligible to play on it. My older sister, Yvonne, was already on the team, and that was all the link I needed. When I got into that new school, one of the first decisions I made was to try out for the basketball team. Already, I had fallen in love with the game.

The summer before, I had started hanging around the little neighborhood parks. They really weren't playgrounds, just little parks. Kids would play basketball there; they also played basketball in backyards, putting up old peach baskets on poles and cutting the bottoms out. Rarely did anybody have a real, official basketball; we used all kinds of balls—rubber balls, old beach balls, tennis balls. But I fell in love with basketball because I could play the game without running around too much, just moving around in one spot a lot, and waiting for my shots. When the school year started, I told my father that I would like to play on the school basketball team. He had this thing about family togetherness, so he told my sister, "Yvonne, you take Wilma along with you to play basketball, you understand?" I think if my sister said no, my father would have told her, "Listen, either Wilma goes along or else you don't play." He felt that strongly about all of us doing things together.

Actually, playing basketball brought out one of the worst personal situations in my family that I can remember. My mother was always very protective of me, because of all of my illnesses, and she would tell me, "Wilma, you rest and take it easy." Then she would go off to work, or to church, or wherever. As soon as she left, I would go out and

41

play basketball. One day, she came home, and she asked me, "What did you do today, Wilma?"

When I said, "I played basketball all afternoon," she hit the ceiling. She told me she didn't want me playing basketball any more, that she didn't want me exerting myself playing games. She really gave me a scolding.

Then, when she wasn't around, I started asking my father if I could play, and he would always say, "Okay, why not?"

One day, my mother came home, and she said, "Wilma, it's not very nice what you're doing, playing your father off against me, getting his permission to play after I already told you no." Then she gave me a terrible spanking, one I'll never forget. The next day, my mother and father had a very bad argument over it, and I felt very bad. I never again played my mother and father off against each other after that.

But in the seventh grade, my mother didn't have any objections to my playing any longer, and my father was all for it. So I went out for the team; I think the coach—his name was Clinton Gray—kept me around just because of my sister. I had an old hand-me-down uniform, and I always sat on the bench, and I never got to play in one single game. But it was fun, anyway. I had the chance to travel from town to town with the team. We played in such places as Gallatin, Tennessee, and in Hopkinsville, Kentucky, and in Murfreesboro, Tennessee. I remember we would sleep on the bus on the way home after games, and even if we got back home at four or five in the morning after a game, we'd all be in school that same morning because nobody wanted to miss a day of school. That whole season, I did nothing but sit on the bench and watch and study everything that was going on on the court. I watched how the rebounders positioned themselves; I studied the rules of the game and how the referees enforced them; I learned such things as how to draw fouls in the act of shooting, and how you get two free throws when you get fouled in the act of shooting and only one otherwise. I used to sit there on the bench and dream about someday becoming a star for this team, but the coach still didn't know I was alive.

I also learned some lessons about what it is like being a girl who loved sports, and about what people thought about such things. There were a lot of distorted views on that subject, and there still are. Down South, there was the old "ladies-don't-do-such-things" way of thinking. You couldn't be a lady and a good athlete at the same time. There was a lot of talk about "playing sports will give you muscles, and you'll look just like a man." They would say, "If you run around too much as a girl you'll never be able to have children." The running was supposed to be too much strain for your body, and your body would never be the same again. Fathers would look at their daughters, and they would say, "Don't do that stuff, it's for the boys."

I hated all of that and always knew, deep inside, that it was a bunch of nonsense. I loved playing in games, and I also loved being a lady after the games. I loved to dress up in pretty outfits just like any other girl. But over half of the girls in the school believed that stuff, and they really didn't want to do a thing. They had this terrible fear that the boys in school just wouldn't look at them if they were athletes. They were afraid of being called tomboys. Instead of playing in games, they did a lot of fashion shows and tap-dancing, even though they really didn't like a lot of that stuff. They did it for show, and to make sure they were considered feminine and not masculine.

A lot of the girls who did play were lazy; they didn't really put their heart into things. They went through the motions, but they never got involved in sports, never forgot the roles they had to play as women or young girls. I never let any of that stuff bother me at all; when I played, I went all out. I was more interested in basketball then than I was interested in boys.

But there was this one boy I did like; everybody called him Robert. Not Bobby, or Bob, But Robert. He was so mean, just a mean little kid, but I knew he liked me. I would be walking home from school, and he'd always be out there, every afternoon, and he'd throw rocks at me as a way of getting my attention. Sometimes, I would change the route, go home a different way, but it made no difference, he'd still be out there, throwing those damned rocks. He was a devil, but an all-right sort of devil, and I liked him. Still, I wasn't obsessed with boys the way a lot of girls were; I was more obsessed with basketball and with improving my game.

So I spent the whole seventh-grade season sitting on the bench, watching and studying and learning. The next year, as an eighth-grader, I thought I might have a chance to do some playing. I was wrong. The coach still treated me as if the only reason I was there was because of my sister. Again, he just ignored me, and I went through another whole season of sitting on the bench. Only difference this time was that he put me in one or two games when we were way behind with only a couple of seconds to go. When I did get in, I would immediately panic and say to myself, "Gee, I'm actually playing, what do I do now?" I did score a basket that season, and I'll never forget it. We were winning big, there were only a couple of seconds left in the game, and somebody threw me the ball. Then everybody started yelling, "Shoot, shoot, shoot." So I shot a one-handed push shot, and it went in. I couldn't believe it.

After that eighth-grade basketball season was over, the coach, Clinton Gray, said to all of us, "Well, I think I'll start another girls' track team." They used to have one years ago, but it was discontinued for some reason or another. He said to us, "Any of you girls on the basketball team are invited. Would any of you like to go out for track?"

I said, "Yes" right away. It would give me something to do after school, just like basketball did, and I liked keeping busy all the time. So the first day the new girls' track team was formed, Coach Gray had us out jogging, just doing nothing else but jogging. It was fun. Then a couple days later, he put us all on a curb, six or seven at a time, and he would stand out there in the middle of the field and he would say, "All right, now, I want all of you to run past me as fast as you can."

The first time I ran in the pack, I noticed that I picked up speed halfway there and I beat everybody else past the coach. Then this continued every day, and every day I'd be the first one past him. But the whole atmosphere at the time was more fun than competition. The track season ran from late March until the end of May, when school got out, and the meets we had that first year weren't meets at all, they were like field days. Playdays, they called them, and they gave out a lot of ribbons and everybody had a lot of fun. I remember our uniforms were old basketball uniforms and sneakers, and all we ever did during practice was jog, every day, from three thirty to four thirty, just jog.

When I came out for the basketball team in the ninth grade, I felt I was really ready to play some. I had spent two years on the bench, and two summers practicing. Sitting on the bench, I became fascinated right away with the way people dribble up the court, their tempos, their gaits, slow or fast. I noticed that if you look into their eyes, you could tell if they were concentrating on handling the ball or else concentrating on what play was coming up. So in practices and in the backyard games, I started stealing the ball like crazy.

If somebody was a slow dribbler, it was easy. The effects were devastating; once you stole the ball on somebody, they'd be embarrassed, and they would start dribbling up the second time with their bodies protecting the ball, and this would throw them off their normal strides, their normal tempos, and the first thing you'd know, they'd try to throw a pass across their body, off the new dribble, and they'd throw it away, or else they'd throw it right at some opposing player, or else they'd throw it in such a way that I'd be able to pick off the pass, too. I realized early that to have the ball stolen from you, in full view of everybody, is demoralizing and will throw off the rest of your game. So I concentrated on watching people dribble, and watching their eyes while they were dribbling, and I made a science out of it for myself. I knew that if I couldn't make the basketball team for any other reason, I'd make it for being able to steal the ball. That's how badly I wanted to play.

But even in that ninth-grade season, when it started, the coach still didn't pay the slightest bit of attention to me. I knew at that point that I was shooting better, rebounding better, and hustling better than most of the girls on the team. But he still paid me no mind. For the first half of that season, I worked like hell in practice, and then I sat on the bench during games. I was angry about that, sitting on the bench, and I started building up my nerve to give the coach a piece of my mind. Finally, at practice one day, I walked over to Coach Gray, and I told him, "Coach Gray, how come I'm not playing?"

There was no response. He didn't even answer me. Then I really got mad. I said, "Coach Gray, I just want you to know that if you put as much time on me as you do on some of these other girls, I'd be a star player on this team."

He laughed at that, and then he said, "Okay, you come to practice tomorrow prepared to do some hard playing."

I did, but nothing really happened. He let me scrimmage some with the first-stringers, but that's about all. I still mostly sat on the bench, and that made it three straight years of sitting on the bench and getting into games with only a couple seconds left and with the team way ahead or way behind. But all the while I was learning, studying, filing things away, and getting madder and madder. I knew that, when my time did come, even though it might take a couple more years, I'd be ready.

When that terrible basketball season ended, I went out for track again, just for something to do. I remember it was cold that spring in Tennessee, and we did a lot of running right in the halls of the school, up and down, turn around, up and down again. Coach Gray told us we have to run, even if it's in the halls of the school, because we have to build up our endurance. When it finally got warm outside, we went out to run, but we never did have a really set program or anything. We did a lot of cross-country type running that spring, over longer distances, but nothing specific.

Coach Gray was a civics teacher at heart; he liked coaching basketball the best, and he formed the girls track team, I think, just to give us something to do and to keep his basketball players in shape. He didn't know the technical aspects of track and field, so he didn't teach us anything. That ninth-grade year, we had a whole bunch of informal-type meets with other schools, the same ones we played in basketball, Springfield, Columbia, and Murfreesboro, Tennessee. They were really disorganized meets, but lots of fun. I ran in five different events that year, the 50, 75, 100, and 200 meters, and on the relay team. I was thirteen years old, a ninth-grader, and believe it or not, I won every race I ran in that season. But the emphasis wasn't on competition in those meets, it was on having fun, and a lot of girls, I suspected, didn't take those meets as seriously as I took them.

Running, at the time, was nothing but pure enjoyment for me. I was winning without really working. I was doing it all on natural ability, and I had no idea about the technical aspects of the sport or even about all the work involved in it. I remember one of those very first meets that year, in Columbia, Tennessee. They didn't even have a track, just a field lined off with lanes. Nobody thought about letting us warm up; they just marched us over to the starting line and pointed straight ahead. I remember the field was all grass, and we were all wearing tennis shoes; I couldn't keep track of the lanes, my breathing patterns were all messed up, and I was nervous to top it all off. The coaches were all standing around, and they were going to wave you over if you swerved into somebody else's running lane.

The 200 that day was the funniest; I still remember it. I remember starting out, and the first thing that happened was that I stepped on this big rock, and then I stepped into this hole and nearly broke my ankle. I kept running straight ahead and I could never see the finish line. That bothered me more than anything, not seeing the finish line. Psychologically, seeing the finish line lets you know how much farther you have to go; it allows you to pace yourself. If you're running straight ahead at full speed with no idea of how far you have to go, you're more liable to burn yourself out.

I won the 200 that day, but I told Coach Gray after the meet, "Coach, I'd rather not run the 200 anymore."

"Why?" he asked.

"Because I can't stand running in anything unless I know where it all ends."

I won about twenty different races that spring, without losing once. But the competition was so informal that they really didn't mean all that much. I don't think winning had any effect on me personally, because I thought of running as little more than an outlet during the spring; I still considered basketball as my favorite sport. But I did say to myself a couple of times, "Gee, Wilma, you're winning at this, and doesn't winning at something feel great? You take running seriously, and you might be a star at something yet." Besides, I loved the feeling of freedom in running, the fresh air, the feeling that the only person I'm really competing against in this is me. The other girls may not have been taking it as seriously as I was, but I was winning and they weren't.

So my ninth-grade year ended, and I had three years of bench-warming in basketball and two years of winning races in track under my belt. Naturally, I still loved basketball better. I was pushing up toward six feet by then, and I had very long arms and legs. I was thinking of myself as a center on the basketball team the next year, or maybe a forward. But that summer, people started talking to me about sports, and they were saying, "Hey, Wilma, maybe you ought to spend more time on running than on basketball. You got to go with your strongest point. . . ."

# 5

# Introduction to Competition

When I went into the tenth grade, I knew I was going to have a chance to really play some basketball that year. My best friend at the time, a girl named Nancy Bowen, felt the same way. The two of us had sat together on the bench for three straight seasons, and we both knew that all of the best players from the team had graduated. So the two of us decided that we were going to make sure that Coach Gray took us seriously. Even before the season started, Nancy and I would go out to the basketball courts at the school playground, and we would talk whoever was there into playing, particularly guys who were playing for the boys' team.

But the turning point for me—and for Nancy, too—came just before the season started, when Coach Gray was in charge of putting on the school's annual minstrel show. He was using the gym for auditions, and for producing the show, which was a lot of tap-dancing and singing basically. So Nancy and I went over to him one day, and we said, "Coach Gray, since the gym is being used anyway, is it all right if we come and shoot some baskets?" He said no. So we decided it was time to switch to Plan B. We both knew that if you could get Coach Gray into a good mood, especially a mood in which he's laughing about the good old days, if you could get him into a mood like that, and then slip the question in on him, he'd say yes to anything. So we went to work on him.

One day, we had him talking for a half hour, laughing, reminiscing, and then we hit him with the question: "Can we come in and shoot?" Finally he said, "All right." So the next day, we showed up with two guys who played on the boys' team, and while Coach Gray was at one end of the gym putting together the minstrel show, we were on the other end, shooting baskets. We were having a good time when, all of a sudden, Coach Gray ordered us out of the gym. He said the dribbling we were doing was interfering with the show. We went, but we weren't finished—not by a long shot. If nothing else, we really put the idea into Coach Gray's head that Wilma Rudolph and Nancy Bowen were pretty serious about playing basketball.

Later, we said to him, "Coach Gray, you know that basketball means more to us than anything else, and we want to be great players, so we have to practice every chance we get." He broke down easier than we ever expected. "Okay," he said, "use the other end of the gym; I'll ignore the dribbling. Just keep the noise down, and no yelling, all right?" All *right*.

So we played every day from about three fifteen

to five in the afternoon, and I'm sure Coach Gray was checking us out of the corner of his eye while he was putting together that minstrel show. As it was, girls had first preference on the gym in the afternoon anyway. This was because David Whitney, the boys' coach, had a soft spot in his heart for girls; he had four daughters of his own. He always used to say, "Girls have a place in life, too." He made his own basketball players come in to practice at night, from around seven to eight, because he wanted the girls to be able to use the gym in the afternoon. For one thing, he used to say he didn't want any of us walking home alone at night so we were to get our practices over with around five or five-thirty.

Then, as it turned out, Coach Gray would pile us all into his little Valiant and take each of us home, right to the front door. They worried about us more than we ever thought. When the basketball season finally did start, a girl named Delma Batson came to live at my house, because she lived in a house about twelve or fifteen miles away from the school and it was easier for her to come home with me after practice than to make that trip. So Nancy and I added Delma to our little crowd and also another girl, Ruth Fletcher, and the four of us became absolutely determined to make our marks on the world through basketball.

We hustled in practice, and we were convinced that all of us would be starters for the varsity, even though we were still only tenth-graders. But Coach Gray was being very secretive. Every day, we would have our lunches, and then we would go down to the gym for what Coach Gray called black-board drills. We would sit around and talk about basketball, and sometimes he would draw plays for us on the blackboard, and show us how to get positioning for rebounds, things like that. But he never gave any of us the slightest inkling of who he had in mind for starters. We used to talk among ourselves, the four of us; we used to say, "Lookit, we're the best and most dedicated players on the team, we have to be starters. How can he pick anybody else?"

So it was the night of the first game already, and still Coach Gray hadn't told us who was starting. We were in the locker room, and we dressed in our uniforms, and then we went out of the floor for warmups. Still nothing. Finally, the buzzer went off, and we all came back to the bench, wondering how much longer can he hold off? Finally, he walked along the bench, and he pulled on the sleeves of our jackets. The jackets he pulled, they were the starters. He pulled mine. He pulled Nancy's. He also pulled Ruth's and Delma's, and that meant all four of us had made the starting team. I was about five-foot-eleven, and I weighed all of about a hundred pounds at the time, and he told me I would be playing guard. Before the season was out, I would be playing forward, too, but it didn't matter that night. I was the happiest person in the whole state of Tennessee, just starting.

That season, we won eleven games and we lost four. The losses were to nonconference teams, and that meant that we won our conference title, the

Middle East Tennessee Conference. I'll never forget my very best game that season. It was a little tournament, a round-robin tournament, held in our high school gym. The games were played during school hours, so all the kids could watch; they could be excused from classes to watch, and that meant that the school gym was packed. It was the first time I ever played before so many of my fellow students—and I didn't miss a single shot or a single free throw. I scored thirty-two points and immediately became a hero in school. That was very important to me, getting the recognition and the attention from my own peers. Usually, the girls' team played games at night; our games were the preliminaries to the boys' games. The crowds were usually mothers and fathers, aunts and uncles; a lot of kids didn't want to spend seventy-five cents to watch basketball games. So on a normal basketball night, there would be just as many adults in the stands as kids, and sometimes there would be more. But that afternoon before the student body of kids, I didn't miss a shot and scored thirty-two points. I was somebody in school after that, for the first time.

Still, that season had its ups and downs. Coach Gray, I remember, had this habit of yelling and screaming at us during times-out, in huddles, in full view of everybody. He gave it to me just like he gave it to everybody else, and I hated that. I hated being yelled at in public. Finally, it reached a head, and I told him, "Don't you yell at me in front of everybody ever again."

He got mad, and he said, "Do it right and I

won't have to yell." I quit on him several times that season—until the next practice. Then I would come back and play harder than anybody else.

Nearly all the coaches of girls' teams back then were men. I only knew one woman coach. Why, I don't know; I guess women back then didn't seriously consider coaching as a career. But Coach Gray was tough; he made us all carry "B" averages in the classroom or else we couldn't play, and he made it clear to us that during basketball season nothing was to interfere with basketball. We had to be dressed and on the practice floor every day at three thirty, no questions asked. He was really dedicated, even though he wasn't paid much more than two hundred dollars extra for being the girls' basketball coach. I can remember that early that season Coach Gray was also a football coach; the football season was still going on, and he would come into the gym to get us started in practice and he'd be wearing football cleats and football pants. I think he would have been a coach for nothing, that's how dedicated he was.

We won our conference title that year, and that meant we earned a spot in the state tournament, the Tennessee High School Girls' Championships. It was played at the Pearl High School in Nashville. Coach Gray made arrangements for us to stay at the house of his sister in Nashville. His sister was married to a university professor, and she just loved having all of us over. She was his favorite sister, and their relationship always reminded me of my relationship with my closest brother, Wesley. All of us were really nervous and excited about playing in the state tournament; it was the first time for all of us, and I was still only a tenth-grader. We won the first game; I scored twenty-six points and Nancy Bowen got thirty. We were elated; we had ourselves convinced we were going to win the whole thing and go down in history as being a real Cinderella team. But we turned into pumpkins instead.

We lost the second game, by seven or eight points, and we were eliminated from the tournament. We played a stupid game that night, made a lot of silly mistakes, and probably deserved to lose. Still, we were all heartbroken. I remember we all cried and cried and cried in the locker room after the game, and we refused to get dressed and go out and watch the rest of the games that night. We all knew that we had hurt Coach Gray by the way we played, making a lot of dumb turnovers and things. And the season was over for us.

What I remember also about that season was this one referee. He worked a lot of our games, and people said he was the track coach at Tennessee State College. His name was Ed Temple. I liked him as a referee because he was always fair; I remember he always called me "Rudolph," never "Number Such and Such" but always by my last name, "Rudolph." Once, after a game that season, he came over to me and said I was lazy. "Rudolph," he said, "you're too lazy to jump." Then he went over to Coach Gray, and he told him the same thing: "Rudolph is lazy." He suggested to Coach Gray that he put a mark up on the wall as a target for me to jump at. He told Coach Gray that I should jump at the target twenty or thirty times every day until I started hitting it. Then he told Coach Gray, "Move the target up on her and make her do it all over again." Sure enough, Coach Gray took his advice, and soon I was jumping twenty, thirty times a day, and that target just kept going up and up and up.

I didn't realize it at the time, and I really didn't realize it until many years later, but Ed Temple was taking an interest in me back then because he had his eye on me for his own track program. He never missed a good prospect; he was always all over the state of Tennessee, refereeing basketball games and watching everybody. He also had a good pipeline back to him; whenever somebody saw a good kid, Ed Temple got the word first. That's why most of the female athletes in Tennessee stayed right in the state and wound up at Tennessee State University.

So it's 1956, and I'm a fifteen-year-old high school sophomore, and my life has never been better. I couldn't remember being happier. School was fun then. I remember the television show "American Bandstand" was very big with the kids, and once a week somebody would come into the school with a bunch of records and we'd have our own "American Bandstand" show after school. They would give out records to kids who won dance contests doing the latest dances, and I even won a couple myself. All the girls were wearing long, tight skirts, the ones that ended just below the knees, and bobby socks and padded bras. They wore chains around their necks with their boyfriends' rings on them, and if you were going steady with an athlete, the girl wore the guy's letter sweaters or their team jackets. Little Richard was big, and Chuck Berry was big, but truthfully, Elvis Presley had no effect whatsoever. Burt High School was all-black, and we just didn't have any kids in the school who identified with Elvis Presley. The black kids sort of knew that he was just a white guy singing black music, but no black kids had motorcycles or leather jackets, probably because they didn't have the money to buy them.

We had all sorts of little social groups in the school, but none that could be described as being like white greasers. One group was the dressers, the kids who came from fairly affluent homes and who showed it off by wearing the best clothes all the time, even to the point where some of the guys in this group came to school wearing suits and ties. The next group was the regulars, the kids who were looked upon as being regular kids, nothing special, just everyday happy kids. Athletes were another group and they usually stuck with other athletes. The funniest group was the "process" guys. They would go to barber shops and get their hair straightened, and everybody would talk about how the barbers used lye to straighten out their hair. Then they would slick back the straightened hair, and this slick look became known as the "Process Look." The guys thought it gave them a worldly image, the image of being real slick dudes who hung around in nightclubs and traveled with the fastest company. But most of them did just the opposite; they traveled with other process guys only.

My whole life at the time revolved around basketball and my family. Robert was my boyfriend; we went out on dates, and when there was nothing else to do, we'd all go hang out at the local teen-age club. Life seemed so uncomplicated, and happy, then.

As soon as the basketball season ended, I had my track stuff on, and I was running. There was a kid in school everybody called "Sundown"; the reason he was called that was because he was so black. His real name was Edward. Anyway, he and I used to skip out of classes almost every day, and we'd sneak off across the street to the municipal stadium, and we'd throw our books over the big wall that surrounded the stadium, then we'd climb the fence and run over to the track and do some running. If we heard any strange sounds, like somebody was coming, we'd run underneath the stands and hide.

Sometimes, when the college track team from Austin Peay College was using the stadium, the place would be filled with these white guys practicing. "Sundown" and I would show up out of the clear blue sky, and they would look, and sort of blink and then go back about their business. The coach of the college team, this white guy, sort of knew that I was skipping out of classes to practice running; he would give me this little wink, like he knew what was going on but like he also had a little bit of admiration for me because I was so in

61

love with running. Whenever he talked to his team, I would sort of hang around on the fringes and listen, hoping to pick up a pointer or two for free. I think he noticed that, too, and when he saw me sort of hanging around, it always seemed he would start talking a little louder than before.

That taste of winning I had gotten the year before never left me. I was more serious about track now, thinking deep down inside that maybe I had a future in the sport if I tried hard enough. So I thought nothing of cutting classes and going out to run. But one day I got a call to report to the principal's office. I went in, and he said, "Wilma, all of us here know just how important running track is to you. We all know it, and we are all hoping that you become a big success at it. But you can't keep cutting classes and going out to run." I was, well, mortified; the principal had found me out. He finally said that if I continued cutting classes, he would have to tell my father, and I knew what that meant. So I stopped. Even so, I was the first girl out there at practice and the last one to leave, I loved it so. We had some more of those playday-type meets early that season, and I kept on winning all the races I was in. I felt unbeatable.

Then came the big meet at Tuskegee, Alabama. It was the big meet of the year. Girls from all over the South were invited down there to run, and the competition was the best for high school kids. It was a whole weekend type of thing, and they had dances and other things planned for the kids when they weren't out running. Coach Gray was going to drive us all down there to Tuskegee Institute, where the meet was held, and I remember we brought our very best dresses. We all piled into his car until there wasn't an inch of empty space in that car. Mrs. Allison, my old teacher, came with us; she was going to chaperon us at the big dance after the meet.

All the way down to Alabama, we talked and laughed and had a good time, and Coach Gray would tell us how tough the competition was going to be, especially the girls from Atlanta, Georgia, because they had a lot of black schools down there, and they had these track programs that ran the whole year because of the warm weather. When we got there, all of us were overwhelmed, because that was the first college campus any of us ever saw. We stayed in this big dorm, and I remember just before the first competition, I started getting this nervous feeling that would stay with me for the rest of my running career. Every time before a race, I would get it, this horrible feeling in the pit of my stomach, a combination of nerves and not eating.

When we got to the track, these girls from Georgia really looked like runners, but I paid them no mind because, well, I was a little cocky. I did think I could wipe them out because, after all, I had won every single race I had ever been in up to that point. So what happens? I got wiped out. It was the absolute worst experience of my life. I did not win a single race I ran in, nor did I qualify for anything. I was totally crushed. The girls from Georgia won everything. It was the first time I had ever tasted defeat in track, and it left me a total wreck. I was so despondent that I refused to go to any of the activities that were planned, including the big dance. I can't remember ever being so totally crushed by anything.

On the ride back, I sat in the car and didn't say a word to anybody, I just thought to myself about how much work was ahead of me and how I would like nothing better in the whole world than to come back to Tuskegee the next year and win everything. When I got home, my father knew immediately what had happened, and he didn't say anything. Every time I used to come home after a meet, I would rush into the house all excited and bubble over with, "I won ... I won." This time I didn't say a word. I just walked in quietly, nodded to my father who was sitting there, and went into my room and unpacked.

After so many easy victories, using natural ability alone, I got a false sense of being unbeatable. But losing to those girls from Georgia, who knew every trick in the book, that was sobering. It brought me back down to earth, and it made me realize that I couldn't do it on natural ability alone, that there was more to track than just running fast. I also realized it was going to test me as a person—could I come back and win again after being so totally crushed by a defeat?

When I went back to school, I knew I couldn't continue to cut classes to practice or else I'd be in big trouble. So I would fake sickness, tell the teacher that I didn't feel well and could I please go home? They would let me go, and then I would go over to the track and run. When that stopped working, when they realized that I looked pretty good for being sick all the time, I simply asked them point-blank, "Look, could I cut this class today and go out and run?" Believe it or not, a lot of teachers said, "Okay, Wilma, go, but don't tell anybody."

I ran and ran and ran every day, and I acquired this sense of determination, this sense of spirit that I would never, never give up, no matter what else happened. That day at Tuskegee had a tremendous effect on me inside. That's all I ever thought about. Some days I just wanted to go out and die. I just moped around and felt sorry for myself. Other days I'd go out to the track with fire in my eyes, and imagine myself back at Tuskegee, beating them all. Losing as badly as I did had an impact on my personality. Winning all the time in track had given me confidence; I felt like a winner. But I didn't feel like a winner any more after Tuskegee. My confidence was shattered and I was thinking the only way I could put it all together was to get back the next year and wipe them all out.

But looking back on it all, I realized somewhere along the line that to think that way wasn't necessarily right, that it was kind of extreme. I learned a very big lesson for the rest of my life as well. The lesson was, winning is great, sure, but if you are really going to do something in life, the secret is learning how to lose. Nobody goes undefeated all the time. If you can pick up after a crushing defeat, and go on to win again, you are going to

65

be a champion someday. But if losing destroys you, it's all over. You'll never be able to put it all back together again.

I did, almost right away. There were more play-days scheduled, and I won all the rest of the races I was in the rest of that season. But I never forgot Tuskegee. In fact, I was thinking that anybody who saw me lose so badly at that meet would write me off immediately. I was wrong. One day, right after the track season ended that year, Coach Gray came over to me and he said, "Wilma, Ed Temple, the referee who is the women's track coach at Tennessee State, is going to be coming down to Clarksville to talk with your mother and father."

"What about?" I asked.

"Wilma," he said, "I think he wants you to spend the summer with him at the college, learning the techniques of running."

# 6

## Learning How to Run

Late that May, Ed Temple did come down from Nashville, and he met with my mother and father. He told them he had this summer track program at the college for promising high school runners, and that he wanted me to be in it. I remember he explained to them all of the rules and regulations that he had in order to put their minds at ease. He had rules like, every girl had to be in by nine o'clock at night, and that none of them were allowed to ride in cars, and none of them were allowed to go into such places as nightclubs. He told them about the full-time equipment manager he had, Pappy Marshall, and how he watched over the girls like a second father, and about Mrs. Perkins, who was a coach in Atlanta and who lived on the same floor with the girls in the dormitory and who kept an eye on them as well. He said all the expenses would be taken care of by the college; the only money we would need would be pocket money, or maybe money for bus fare to visit home. My father did not want me to leave home because I was so young but he finally agreed. So I spent the next week or so packing, getting my things ready, rearranging my suitcase, and waiting. Finally, Coach Temple called and said he would be down to pick me up and drive me to the college himself.

I remember the ride up to Nashville; Coach Temple and I talked about basketball the whole time, not track, basketball. He talked about all of his refereeing, and about the girls he saw play who he thought were good. When we got there, he took me to my room at Wilson Hall, and a lot of girls were already there, girls who were staying in the dorm to go to summer school. One by one, the other track girls started coming in, and each of us got a roommate, and the older girls sort of looked after the younger ones. I was the youngest one there, I soon discovered. The younger girls were always following the older ones around, looking up to them, asking advice, and so on. We had certain do's and don't's in the dorm, like no cooking in the rooms. My roommate turned out to be a girl named Martha Hudson, and we immediately became good friends; before the summer was over, she was coming home with me on visits to my house.

So all the track girls settled in over the weekend, and on the first Monday morning, we went down to see the equipment manager, Pappy Marshall, and he issued us everything we would need. We each got a couple of T-shirts, a couple pair of shorts, a couple of sweatsuits, and heavy Converse basketball sneakers to run in. This was on purpose, and it would be a couple of weeks before we were issued our first pair of track shoes.

The next morning, we were roused out of bed a little before six, to do our first running. It was cross-country, and we would run a good six miles. We would run from about six in the morning to eight in the morning, then come back in for breakfast. We would rest after breakfast until about ten thirty and then go out and run another six miles and come in for lunch. After lunch, we would rest up until about three in the afternoon, and then we would do the six miles again.

So, the routine settled in on us quickly: we were running about twenty miles a day, five days a week. It was all cross-country running, over hills and farmlands mostly, and there were these big oil tanks way out in the distance and we would run out to them, and this became known as "going to the tanks." On weekends, we went to the movies, and to church, and we rested.

After the first two weeks, the cross-country phase was over. Coach Temple explained to us that all of the cross-country running was for the purpose of building up our endurance. Then we started in on running different distances, and we started learning the various techniques of proper running. I can remember learning some of the basics of running right there, how to smooth out, how to stop fighting yourself, keeping the fists loose. That is a very small thing, but a very important thing. The less tense your muscles are, the better you can run; if you are running with clenched fists, it's an indication that the rest of your body is tight, too. Run with open hands and, chances are, the rest of you is just as loose. Some girls were running while leaning backwards, and this was no good. You've got to lean into your race, not away from it. We walked through everything dozens of times before we ran through it.

Always, Coach Temple kept things on a team basis; we were a team, not just a bunch of individuals. He kept the motivation high because under the team concept all of us became very competitive. In fact, the competition among us that summer was about as intense as any competition I can ever remember. Still, we all stayed friends.

Myself, all of the cross-country running did me a lot of good. It built up my stamina, and it got me to breathing free and easy, naturally. So when I finally started running the 100, or the 200, I didn't have to worry about my breathing patterns, they just came naturally. I learned certain tricks of breathing—taking long, deep breaths, take air in and let it out; doing this a couple of times relaxes everything. We also learned certain exercises that loosen up the body, make the arms and legs feel as light as feathers.

The goal in all of this is relief; before a race, say, everybody naturally tenses up, the mind is tense, the body is tense, and you need relief from this tension any way you can get it. I could never eat before a race, and I would get this horrible feeling in the pit of my stomach, and it would never go away, it seemed. Sometimes, I would vomit, or get this vomiting feeling. This form of tension stayed with me my entire career, and no matter what I did I could never get relief from it.

That summer, I also came face to face with another thing that would stay wih me for my entire career: bad starts. I always had trouble with starts. For one thing, I had very bad reflexes on starts, and for another thing, my long legs made starts very awkward for me. I had no speed coming out of the starting blocks, and it took me longer to get any kind of acceleration going because of this. I tried a lot of different things to compensate, but nothing really worked. I tried blocking everything out of my mind except the starter's gun, but I still couldn't improve myself out of the blocks. That meant that I was always better in something like the 100 or 200 than I was in something like the 50 meter. Heck, I needed forty-five feet or so just to get started.

I had never worked with starting blocks before until that summer, and they gave me hell the whole time. There was so much of me to come out of the blocks that I never felt comfortable. I was just too tall. I would come out and I'd be wobbling, and my first five or six strides would always be off. But that also taught me another lesson about running: every runner is different, and every runner has different problems. What was a problem for me, starting blocks, was no problem for a lot of other girls; but, on the other hand, what bothered them, not being able to deliver a good finishing kick, never bothered me.

I remember that summer, Coach Temple put on this Blue and White meet. He split all of us up into Blue teams and White teams, and he conducted a real meet. He held regular races and events, kept score, the whole thing. When kids around campus heard there was going to be a Blue and White meet, they'd all turn out to watch, because they knew this would be better than the average track meet. The competition was very keen.

The day of the meet, the football seats were packed, the crowd was bigger than turned out for most meets against other schools. I remember running a couple of races that day, not winning, but beating a couple of girls who were college runners and I felt good about that because I was only fifteen years old and still in high school. Coach Temple didn't say much to any of us that summer, but that was his way. He never said very much. We found out if he didn't say anything to you, you were doing all right. If he started saying things to you, that usually meant you were in trouble.

He put together this junior relay team that summer, and I was on it. Four high school girls. We wound up so good that we were giving the senior team a run every time out. They'd beat us, but every time the margin got smaller, six yards, five yards, four yards. We started getting cocky, and we'd tell the senior team, "If you don't want to get shown up today, you'd better be ready to run." But still, looking back on it, I think one of the reasons we didn't beat them outright was because the four of us were holding back a little, in our heads. It was like, you know, they were older than us, more experienced, and we didn't want to be disrespectful. We also wanted to be liked by the older girls, and there was no quicker way to become disliked than to start beating them.

This junior relay team did the 440, and each of us had 110 meters to run. That was another trick of Coach Temple's—every distance was in meters instead of yards. He used to explain to us that in the Olympics everything is meters, and what sense does it make for us to run yards? After a while I came to love running with this relay team more than anything else; the distance was right for me, the girls were right, and we were winning. It was the perfect combination.

That junior relay team consisted of Martha Hudson, my roommate, and Willi White and Annette Anderson, besides myself. That summer, we knew we were good, and we knew right off that Coach Temple was preparing us to run in the National AAU meet in Philadelphia at the end of the summer. So we even had a goal: win the AAU.

As the weeks went by at the summer program, I felt better and better; I had a lot of visitors on weekends—Robert, who was my boyfriend by now; my high school coach; my brothers and sisters. At night, we hung out in the college recreation hall, and generally we killed time by playing this card game called Bid-Wist, which is black people's bridge. It's a game that's a little bit like bridge, and also like spades; you bid, and you keep score, and you play for hours. It's a status game among blacks, just like bridge is among whites. We never bet money; the joy of playing had to do with winning. You had a partner, two people played against two people, and the challenge was in outmaneuvering the others with the cards. Money was not even a factor; we never thought about it.

So, the rest of that summer was spent perfecting the relay routine. We eventually realized that the key to being a good relay team is in having good judgment as far as your partners are concerned. You have to know them, their moves, their reactions, their thinking, their reflexes. You have to know them as people. You have to know who is fast, who is a little slow on the handoff, whose reflexes are just a second or two off. Then you compensate for it. All of this takes time, and it works toward precision. You go through the whole relay routine so many times your head spins; you walk through it first, then jog through it, go through it in a slow-motion routine, then at various speeds before you finally go into it full speed.

Something like passing the baton; that takes weeks to perfect, weeks to get down, and even then it might be off. Passing the baton is one of the most important things to running on a relay team. If a baton is dropped, it is the passer's fault automatically, no matter what happens. The reason the passer is responsible is because the receiver can't ever see the baton, can't ever see the maneuver of passing it because she's poised straight ahead, concentrating on taking off. It's the passer's job to get the baton into her hand. The receiver, as soon as she feels the baton, she's off and running; she starts gripping and running immediately. So the passer has to put it in the right place—right in the middle of her grip on the first try.

That means if you're coming in fast, you have to learn to cut your stride so you can make a perfect handoff without losing any ground in the process by slowing down. It is tricky. I ran every leg on that relay team except the first because I was having these awful problems with the starts. Coach Temple knew right off that I was going to have this problem for a while, but he also knew right off that I was very good at catching people from behind. It seemed whenever I was running from a position that was behind somebody else, I always caught them.

So in the weeks before the National AAU meet, we worked on the relay team until we closed in on perfection. I settled in on the anchor leg, and the more we ran, the more confident we became. The meet was going to be held in Philadelphia, and that's all we talked about.

Finally, a couple of days before the meet, Coach Temple lined up this caravan of station wagons, and we all piled into them, and off we went toward Philadelphia. I rode with him, and I got to sit in the front seat, right next to him, because my legs were so long it would have been unbearably uncomfortable to sit cramped up in the back seat. He made me the navigator, handed me a bunch of road maps, and then rode me all the way there because I couldn't get any directions right. But I even learned something on that trip—I learned how to read road maps. I learned by trial and error, but I learned anyway.

We stayed in a big hotel in Philadelphia, and it was the first time I had ever stayed in one in such a big city. Everything in Philadelphia seemed so foreign to me; the buildings seemed so big, so awesome, I was intimidated. When we went to the stadium—Franklin Field—I nearly fainted. I had never seen a stadium that big before, and I actually felt like a midget.

Coach Temple had entered me in three events in the meet, the 75-, the 100-, and the 440-relay. In that meet, there were two trials, and then the finals, to whittle the fifty or sixty girls in each event down to the final six or eight. So we started running qualifying heats at around nine in the morning, and the meet didn't end until the sun started going down around six at night. It was the toughest day of my life up to that point, but it was also the most productive. I ran in nine races that day, and I won them all. I won both qualifying heats in the 75, then won the final big. I won both heats in the 100, and then won the final there, too. Our crack relay team won both of its qualifying heats, then we won the final, too.

So I was nine for nine, and we girls from Tennessee State swept the whole junior division of the National AAU meet and all we had were five girls running in the junior events. But there was no overwhelming reaction from the crowd, and there was nothing in the papers the next day, because that's the way it was for us in girls' track and field at the time. Especially if you were running in the juniors; the seniors had a tough enough time getting anybody to pay attention to them, getting any recognition, any publicity. The juniors forget it. I won nine races that day, and our team won the junior title, and none of us even thought about looking in the sports pages the next day for writeups because we knew auto-

76

matically that nobody would bother to write us up. It was like, oh, well, girls' track, that's not really a sports event.

During the meet, I remember, we had what was like our own little encampment, where all of us hung out when we weren't running. They were calling events all over the place, on the loudspeaker, semifinals for the 100-yard dash, finals for the 75, and you could never keep track of what was going on yourself. So after you ran, you came right back to your team camp, and when you were called to run again, Coach Temple, would get you up and off. I remember coming off the track after one of the trial heats, and going to the little camp, and Coach Temple said, "Nice, Wilma, nice race, take off your shoes and rest now." I no sooner got my shoes off, Coach Temple is up and he says, "Wilma, get going, the quarter finals of the 100 are coming up." My shoes were off and my feet rested for all of about three seconds.

Coach Temple was funny during that meet. He didn't say very much, even though his girls were running away with everything. He was very reserved, in control, keeping track of which girls belonged where at what moment. He didn't scream and yell at anybody, never once got excited. When he wasn't telling us to get going to this heat, or to take our shoes off, he was telling us, "The tea and honey is over there, drink some."

We stayed over that night, it was a Saturday night, but there was no big victory party, or celebration, or anything like that. In fact, the only reason we stayed over in the first place was because the seniors were running the next day, and we were to go back with them on Sunday night. Coach Temple wasn't very big on celebrations anyway. He took us to dinner that night, as he always did, but that was about it. It was as if he had expected us to win, and there was no big deal because we had. He didn't say anything to me; he mentioned something like, "You're coming along real well, Wilma, you've got a lot of potential." But he certainly didn't say, "Congratulations," or "Sensational," or "Way to go," or anything like that. It was not his style. In fact, the only people in the whole place who seemed excited that I won nine races, or that the team won the junior title, were the other girls on the team. Other than that, nobody really paid any attention.

But for me, personally, I think that weekend turned the whole Tuskegee episode around for me. I won nine races, and I was confident again, and those victories helped wipe out the memory of those losses earlier. I was looking forward to going home, to sharing it all with my mother and father, the people who counted. I knew they would be as happy as I was, and I knew they would appreciate what it meant to me to win again, after Tuskegee.

The last thing I remember about that weekend at the Nationals was one of the meet directors coming over to Coach Temple, and telling him, "Coach, we've got two big celebrities here, baseball players. One is Jackie Robinson and the other is Don Newcombe, and they both play for the Brooklyn Dodgers. Can you bring a couple of your girls down to get their pictures taken with these two baseball players?"

So Coach Temple picked out a couple of us; I was one of them, and they led us all down to this little platform where Jackie Robinson and Don Newcombe were standing. I was kind of shy, embarrassed to say anything because I was afraid to have people listen to me talk because of my Southern accent. I was ashamed of it when I was with people who weren't from Tennessee; I didn't want them to think of me as some kind of foreigner. With people from Tennessee, it didn't matter. But anyway, they brought us over to Jackie Robinson and Don Newcombe.

I never in a million years thought I'd have to talk to them, just stand there and get my picture taken. But out of nowhere, all of a sudden, Jackie Robinson started talking to me. He said, "I really like your style of running and I really think you have a lot of potential." Then he asked me what grade I was in, and what part of Tennessee I was from, and how long I had been running? So I had to answer him. He looked genuinely shocked when he told me I was still in high school. Then, he said, "You are a fascinating runner and don't let anything, or anybody, keep you from running. Keep running." After the pictures were taken, I went back and I was overwhelmed. All the way back to Tennessee, I thought about Jackie Robinson, and what he said, and for the first time in my life I had a black person I could look up to as a real hero. Jackie Robinson, after that day, was my first black hero.

# 7

## The Olympic Trials

Right after Philadelphia, and just before my junior year in high school, Coach Temple and I had a long talk; it was the first time he talked to me about the Olympic Games. He said, "Wilma, I think you have a chance to run in the Olympics, and I think you should give it a try.

At the time, I had no real idea of what the Olympics were; I had no idea the games consisted of competition among countries of the world. I thought they were just some big track meet somewhere. Coach Temple told me the 1956 games would be held in Melbourne, Australia, and that didn't ring a bell at all because I had never heard of Melbourne. But I was excited and I was willing to give it a try if Coach Temple wanted me to. He told me not to worry about getting into any special shape, not to worry about any special training, because after all that I had been through during the summer, I was in shape already. He said, "Wilma, the Olympic Trials are coming up in about two weeks, and I'm taking a bunch of my college girls up to Seattle, Washington, where the trials are going to be held, and I want you to come with us."

I never hesitated. Before I even knew it, there I was, a sixteen-year-old high school junior in a car with a bunch of college stars driving to Seattle, Washington, for the Olympic Trials. Coach Temple drove; I sat next to him in the front seat, and the other girls with us, I remember, were Margaret Mathews, Isabelle Daniels, Willi White, Lucinda Williams, and Mae Faggs, who was the senior girl on the team and the person most responsible for me becoming a competitive runner, after Coach Temple.

Mae Faggs was like a second coach to me. At the time, Mae held all sorts of United States' records in women's track; she had won medals in the Olympics already. She was the one everybody else looked up to, and she took a special interest in me right from the very first day I met her, and that interest stayed for years after. On the way to the trials with Coach Temple, we stopped often to eat, and Mae and I talked a lot. She always seemed to be telling me, without really coming out with it in so many words, that the time to start performing as an individual is now and to stop worrying about fitting in with everybody else, stop worrying about whether or not so-and-so is still going to like me if I win that race. I always seemed to be concerned about that—not losing friends. She used to hide her real message in a nice way; she'd say things like, "Wilma, you really have the ability to perform as an individual." At first, I wondered what she was talking about, but then it started sinking in—performing as an individual. An *individual*. Up to that point, all I was concerned about was fitting in with all the rest of the girls.

We all had a real great trip up from Nashville to Seattle. Coach Temple took us to the very best restaurants, the very best motels; we lived first class the whole way. For Mae Faggs and I to become such close friends along the way was unusual, I'd say. She was an established star, and I was just a high school kid. I was pushing six feet in height, and she was all of four foot ten, so her stride was much smaller than mine; it seemed as if I could take four steps to her every one. Yet every time we raced that summer, I felt that I could beat her, but I never really wanted to. Finishing second to Mae was all that mattered.

I think she sensed that I had been holding back, purposely avoiding beating her, and her idea was for me to get more selfish and start beating everybody I could beat, regardless of who they were. I think Coach Temple noticed the same tendency on my part, and the reason he put me on the relay team in the first place was because I failed to win a race when I should have. Usually, you get picked for winning. In this case, I got picked for not winning.

We were running a relay leg that summer at Tennessee State, and I was running the same leg as Isabelle Daniels. It was the anchor leg, and we both got the batons at the very same moment. From then on, I matched her stride for stride, and I realized, for the very first time, that I could pull away from her any time I really wanted to. But I didn't. Just knowing that I could was enough for me. So I held back and let her win. There was no advantage for me in beating her, because it would have caused hard feelings; I thought if you're a high school kid you don't go around showing up established stars by beating them.

But Coach Temple sensed that I had held back on purpose, and from that day on, he put me on relay teams. He told me later that a coach knows his runners like a teacher knows his students. He said he knew that I could have won that race, but didn't on purpose. He never said a word about it at the time, but all I knew was that he had entered me in both the 200 meters and on a relay team for the Olympic Trials.

When we got to Seattle, it was very cold, and this threw me off a little bit. I had been used to running in very hot weather down in Tennessee. We had a couple days before the trials began, and we got used to the cold by simply walking around in it. We really didn't do anything for those days but lounge around in the university dormitory we were staying in, and walk the streets. About fifty or sixty girls were there for the trials, and as time passed, I started to get that horrible feeling in the pit of my stomach; I started getting nauseated, and I couldn't eat a thing. Finally, Mae Faggs came over to me, and she said, "Skeeter Baby"— that was my nickname, "Skeeter," because with my long arms and legs I looked like a mosquito— "Skeeter Baby, you want to make the United States Olympic team?"

I said, "I sure do."

Then she said, "All right, all you have to do to make this team is stick with me. Put everything else out of your mind and concentrate on doing nothing else but sticking with me. You stick with me in the race, you make the team."

I decided that was the best way of going about it. Especially after we had a couple of workouts in the stadium. The place looked so big to me I was intimidated and couldn't imagine what it would be like with all of those seats filled with people. So: we get to the first trial heat of the 200 meters, and I'm entered in the race with Mae. I'm at the start, and I'm thinking about what she had said, and nothing else.

I remember the gun going off, and I remember taking off with a good start, and when I looked up, I saw that I had actually passed Mae and was ahead of her. We finished in a dead heat, the same time and everything, and she was happier than I was about that. She rushed over to me, and she was bubbling over with happiness: "Skeeter Baby, you know what? I told you to stick with me, I didn't tell you to beat me." Then she hit me with a bombshell. She said, "You know, as soon as this thing is over, I'm going to retire. I think you've made it, you're ready to replace me right now. You really beat me in that race. What took you so long to get there? We've all known you had it in you, but we all wondered when it would come out. Today it did."

So I had qualified for the United States Olympic team. Mae stayed on me for the rest of the trials and for days after, telling me to run as an individual and don't worry about the team. "You run well yourself, that's how you help the team." I did get that feeling for the first time in that race against Mae that ended in a dead heat.

From that moment on, it seemed as if I wasn't afraid to challenge anybody anywhere. Whatever fears I had, fears of offending somebody else by beating them, fears of being rejected by my teammates if I did too well, all of those fears vanished. My confidence as a runner had reached an all-time high, and my confidence as a person was improving, too. When we got back to Tennessee State, I noticed that everybody was excited; people kept coming around to wish me well. I even got my first writeup in a newspaper when I got back; the Nashville paper did a story on me.

Back home in Clarksville, things were happening, too. Some people in town were excited that I had made the Olympic team; they also knew that my mother and father didn't have very much money, and they wouldn't be able to afford to buy me new clothes, and they probably thought I didn't even have luggage to put anything in. They were right. These people eventually called Coach Gray, and they told him, "Bring Wilma downtown, let her buy some clothes and some luggage so she can go to Melbourne in style, and we'll take care of everything." They did, and I have never forgotten those people to this day. I love them dearly for the help they gave me when I most needed it.

Coach Temple took care of all of the personal

arrangements for me. He got my passport in order, I remember, and he gave it to Mae Faggs to put in her bags so I wouldn't lose it. He said, "Wilma, you lose this little thing, you might never get back home. So I'm giving it to Mae for safekeeping." The people in Clarksville even had a little send-off ceremony for me when I left town to start Olympic training.

My first stop as the youngest member of the 1956 United States Olympic team was Los Angeles. We were going to have a two-week training camp prior to leaving for Australia. I remember that trip distinctly because it was the first time I had ever flown in an airplane. I can remember sitting there, and the stewardess coming around and asking me, "What would you like to eat?"

I said, "Nothing." I thought that I would have to pay for the food, so I said no. I didn't have any money for things like food on airplanes. Mae Faggs finally came over and told me very quietly that I didn't have to pay for anything, that the food was free. So I ordered, but didn't touch a thing because I was so nervous. The tray sat there in front of me, with all of the food on it, and the other girls kept coming by and picking off whatever they wanted, the rolls, the desert, the tomatoes.

When we got to Los Angeles, we were put into a hotel downtown and told that a bus would take us every day to practice at the field at the University of Southern California. What I remember best about my first look at Los Angeles was the smog; back in 1956, the smog there was so bad, I

*Six-year-old Wilma Rudolph poses with her older sister Yvonne.*
(WIDE WORLD)

*Mae Faggs and Wilma Rudolph finish 1-2 in the Washington, D.C., trials for the U.S. Women's Olympic Track Team, 1956.*
(WIDE WORLD)

*Tennessee State Track Coach Ed Temple with his Olympic team including Wilma (far left), before leaving for Australia, 1956.* (WIDE WORLD)

*Wilma sets a new Olympic record in the Women's 100 Meter Event, Rome, 1960.* (U.P.I.)

*Wilma wins!* (U.P.I.)

*Her third Olympic gold medal—winning the Women's 400 Meter Relay Race, Rome, 1960. (U.P.I.)*

*The Olympic spirit—Wilma with Britain's Dorothy Hyman and Italy's Giuseppina Leone. (U.P.I.)*

*Wilma returns home triumphant, with her parents, Blanche and Ed Rudolph, and sister Charlene.* (WIDE WORLD)

*The parade of honor in Nashville.* (U.P.I.)

*President Kennedy chats with Wilma, her mother and school chum, Robert Logan, 1961.* (U.P.I.)

*Wilma in action, 1961.* (U.P.I.)

*Wilma Rudolph trades her track shoes for a diploma from Tennessee A & I University, May, 1963.* (U.P.I.)

remember saying to myself, "The weather here is great, too bad you can't see anything."

The coach of the U.S. women's track team that year was Nel Jackson, who was the coach at Tuskegee. She was the first black women's coach ever for the U.S. Olympic team. Since two weeks wasn't all that much time to get acquainted with a whole team, she relied on each of the girls' coaches for information. For example, Coach Temple would write out training techniques for each of us, and he would give them to Mae Faggs, the senior girl from Tennessee State, and she would give them to Coach Jackson to follow. We trained every day, every morning, regular workouts. But the truth was that training for the United States Olympic team was even easier than what I had already been through training at Tennessee State. The competition among the girls wasn't as keen as it was back at Tennessee State and it was more businesslike in Los Angeles.

I met a lot of people during those two weeks, and one I remember to this day is Dan Ferris, a very nice man from the Amateur Athletic Union. He made sure that all of us were taken care of and that we had everything we needed; he was friendly and polite to us, like a very nice grandfather. I remember sitting around in the hotel at night, and Mae Faggs explaining to me everything there was to know about the Olympic Games. Simple, basic things. I remember asking her what the five Olympic rings meant, and she explained that they symbolized five continents linked together in friendly competition. She told me that this was her third Olympics, and that she valued the knowledge she acquired from traveling and the friendships she made with people from other countries more than she valued the medals she won. "You'll see, Wilma," she said, "you'll see what I mean."

We were not told about the other teams in the Olympics, nobody gave us any scouting reports on the Russians, or anything like that. All we did was concentrate on ourselves, the United States team. I was running very well at the time, particularly with the 440 relay team. Mae Faggs was running the first leg, Margaret Mathews was number 2, I was number 3, and Isabelle Daniels was anchor. We were confident during the two weeks in Los Angeles that we were going to do something in Melbourne. In fact, I was more excited about running with that relay team than I was about running the 200 meters; I would pay for that, as it turned out. When we broke training camp in Los Angeles, we were assigned to travel with the men's track team, but the fellow who looked after me most was Bill Russell, who was the captain of the men's basketball team. He used to watch over me like I was his daughter; he knew I was the youngest person on the U.S. team and he wanted to make sure nothing happened to me. He was beautiful.

Finally, the day arrived when we took off for Melbourne. The airplane was packed with athletes of all kinds, and they were jumping around all over the plane and having a good time for themselves. A lot of them played cards, and I wandered around the airplane watching the various games. Some of the athletes took their blankets and folded them up and made little beds for themselves between the seats and just slept. It was going to be a two-day flight from Los Angeles to Melbourne, and the first leg of it was from LA to Hawaii. We stopped in Hawaii for the night and, when we got off in Honolulu, I couldn't believe my eyes. The dancing girls were there to greet us, and they all had flowers for us, and kisses. Then I saw the tropical setting of Hawaii, the ocean and the palm trees, and I thought this must be a fantasy world.

But I'll never forget what happened on the main street of Honolulu when we were allowed to go out to do some shopping. There were three of us from the girls' track team, three black girls from the South, and we were walking down the main street downtown, window shopping. We came upon this white woman with a little dog. When the woman saw us coming, she looked at us with this horrified look, and then she picked up her little dog and walked across the street with it, and put it down again. She looked at us from across the street with this look that said, "What are you natives doing out in the street?" I never thought I would run into racial prejudice in such a beautiful place as Hawaii, but I did, and that made me sad for the rest of that day. We all felt sad, because here we were, as members of the United States Olympic team, and that didn't really matter at all because we were still black, no matter what we did. After the night in Hawaii, we all loaded up in the airplane again and headed for the second stop, the Fiji Islands.

Now, the Fiji Islands intrigued me. I had never before seen a whole island of totally black people. Everybody was black, the airport workers, the taxi drivers, the policemen—I remember the policemen wore these skirts with bamboo hats. The heat was incredible. I remember getting off the plane and walking smack into the heat, and it almost knocked me over. We had been flying so long that we all wanted to get out of the plane and stretch a little, but the heat was so oppressive we all decided that another nap on the plane would be better. I didn't see any buildings at all, just thatched-roof huts, and I wondered why nobody had built any buildings. After all, even Clarksville had buildings.

Another thing about the Fiji Islands was the language. Though the people were all black, none of them spoke English. That amazed me at the time, and it really got me to thinking about how many people live on this planet, how many different people there are, speaking different languages. All of the black people I knew back home spoke English, and they had Southern accents; but here in Fiji were black people speaking a different language with no accents. I began to realize that the world was bigger than Clarksville, or even Tennessee, and I said to myself, "You're lucky, you're luckier than all of the kids back home, because you're getting to see all of these things and they're not." And I started to realize a little about what Mae Faggs had told me about the knowledge you get from traveling, and how she valued that more than her Olympic medals.

When we took off from the Fiji Islands, the next stop was Melbourne itself. We all settled back, because this was going to be the longest leg of the trip. I looked out of the window of the airplane, and I looked down at the Pacific Ocean, and I remember saying to myself, "Is this all one big dream? What am I, Wilma Rudolph, a sixteen-year-old kid from Clarksville, Tennessee, doing on this airplane going to Melbourne, Australia, for the Olympic Games?" How could I believe what was happening to me? It was only a couple of years ago that I couldn't even walk right, must less run. It was only a couple of years ago that I was going back and forth from Clarksville to Nashville for treatments on my leg. Now here I was on this big chartered jet going off to another country as one of the fastest women in the whole world. I had these thoughts running through my head as I dozed off. I was awakened by the voice of the stewardess over the intercom; she was saying, "Ladies and gentlemen, please fasten your seat belts. We're preparing to land in Melbourne...."

# 8

## Melbourne

Melbourne, Australia. It was in October, 1956, that we landed in Melbourne to compete in the seventeenth modern Olympiad. The very first thing I noticed there were the accents of the people, very stiff and formal British accents. But the city itself was not too much different from a lot of cities I had seen in America. When we checked into the Olympic Village, where all the athletes live, I was overwhelmed by the different kinds of people, so many different kinds, Orientals, Europeans, Africans, Mexicans. But as we started to meet these people, we realized that they were there for the same two reasons we were—to win and to meet new people. Everybody there, it seemed, was fascinated by America. People would stop us all over the Olympic Village, and other athletes would stop us, and they would say that their secret desire in life was to visit America.

I was asked for my first autograph at the Village, and no matter what anybody says, it does make you feel important and nice, when somebody asks you for your autograph. After a while, all of us girls on the U.S. team would spend an hour every day outside the gate of the Village, signing autographs for whoever wanted them. We did that because we wanted to, not because anybody told us to. We felt it would be a small gesture of goodwill that would make us a lot of new friends, and it sure did. So many people wanted the autographs of Americans that we usually wound up staying more than just an hour, and once or twice we signed for almost two hours.

Although it was fall in America, it was summer in Australia at the time, and that meant that we had to get used to hot weather again. We had a week to train and get used to the surroundings, but I remember saying to myself, "Gee, if this is summer, it must be a pretty cold summer because this isn't like summer in Tennessee." I actually thought it was cold over there, and I can't remember once being warm while out of doors. The food was absolutely delicious. Another thing about that week that I remember was the starting drills. The starter of the games, an Australian, would visit every team's training session once, and he would run through a regular start so everybody had an idea of what was coming. He had this peculiar British accent, and when he visited the American practice he did tell us one of the reasons he was there was for all of us to get a chance to hear him talk. He said he didn't want anybody getting off to bad starts and losing races because they didn't understand him. At practice itself, we didn't have a regular schedule, but we were out there every day for a week, running.

The women's compound at the Village was very

93

secluded, and the rules were similar to the rules Coach Temple had. Every girl had to be in by nine o'clock at night, and no men were allowed to visit in their rooms. Actually, if people want to know the real truth, most of the girls in the compound weren't all that interested in men at that point; they were there for one reason, to do their very best, and maybe win, in the Olympics. You figure, most of them had already spent three or four years training very hard to get to the Olympics, and many of them had to survive in trials and qualifying meets, and they weren't about to mess all of that up and throw it away by sneaking some guy into their room and probably getting disqualified from the games. The trick was to concentrate and work very hard prior to the competition. Then, when the competition was over for you, you could relax or unwind, celebrate or be consoled, by men. But I remember it was strictly business for the girls before they competed.

I ran with the relay team every day in practice, and we all felt that we'd be in the top three. Mostly, we felt it was motivation among us that would do the job. We knew each other well, and it was up to us to get everybody else on the ball. If one of us was letting down a little in practice, somebody would jump on her and get her moving. There was concern about our baton-passing. Frankly, it wasn't very good, and we were doing it all on just plain blinding speed. Coach Temple was not there in Australia, and had he been, he would have been all over us for the way we were passing the baton. The timing wasn't down, and we were sloppy. I do think there was a psychological letdown in not having Coach Temple there; all of us sort of felt it. I know that if he had been there, we would have been concentrating more. Just having him there, even as a spectator, would have meant something to us. He gave us this feeling of security, just being around. So there was an empty spot for us, but none of us were admitting it, even though we all felt it.

The opening parade gave me a good feeling; it was the first time I had ever seen one, and here I was, right in the middle of it. After it, I met Betty Cuthbert. She was the star of the whole show, the runner to beat, the best runner in Australia, the hometown favorite on top of everything else. We talked for a good long while, mostly about shoes— track shoes. She said that the United States still had not developed a good track shoe for its women runners, and then she showed us the Australian shoes, which she considered the best. They were. They were made from this very soft kangaroo leather, and they were very light and looked pretty in white. We were all jealous right away. We all wanted them, and we felt these shoes were giving the Australian runners a little edge that we didn't have. Betty Cuthbert picked up our feelings right away, and she said, "Look, I know exactly where you can get shoes made for you just like this, right here in Melbourne." The shoes, she said, would cost between twenty and thirty dollars a pair. I wanted them desperately, but I couldn't afford them and I knew it. Mae Faggs offered to loan me the money to buy a pair, but I didn't want to take it because I knew when I got home my mother and father would have to pay her back, and I didn't think they had the money to do so. So I just ate my heart out.

My very first Olympic race was three days into the games. It was the trial heat in the 200. I don't remember a single person I ran against because I blocked everything out of my mind except getting there and qualifying. They were taking the first three finishers in that heat and moving them on to the semifinals. I finished third and made it. In the semis, they took the first two. This is where I blew it. I really don't know what happened, except that I did not run as fast as I should have. I finished third and was eliminated from the 200.

I felt terrible after; I couldn't eat or sleep. I felt as if I had let down everybody back home and the whole United States of America. I asked myself over and over, "How will I ever be able to face them again back home? I'm a failure." I didn't go out of my room, I just sat there and felt miserable. I tried to tell myself they were just faster, nothing you can do about that. People would drop in and try to make me feel better, but that never worked either, because who wants to feel better at a time like that? You're better off feeling miserable and getting it out of your system once and for all.

In the back of my mind, I kept telling myself, "You'll have another chance, you'll get to redeem yourself in the relay." A couple days later, I forced myself to go to the Olympic Stadium and watch Betty Cuthbert run—she won the 100, 200, and 400 for three gold medals. I sat there in the stands watching her, and I said to myself, "You've got four years to get there yourself, but you've got to work hard for those four years and pay the price."

Watching her win those gold medals motivated me into making a commitment to do the very same thing someday. I was determined that four years from then, no matter where the Olympics were held, I was going to be there and I was going to win a gold medal or two for the United States. Meanwhile, I still had the chance to help win one for the United States in the relay. Watching Betty Cuthbert win snapped me out of my blue mood, and I was determined to give my very best effort in the relay to salvage something, not only for the U.S. team but for myself.

On the day of the relay, Mae Faggs was at her best. She was the motivator for us. We were all nervous; I'm sure she was just as nervous as we were, but she never once showed it. She was very good at having a calm and cool exterior when she was nervous. She really psyched us up that day; she went around telling us, "Let's go get 'em, let's give it all we've got, let's make it into the top three and win ourselves a medal." Soon, we all started picking up on that, and we were actually hyper, telling ourselves that we really were about ready to go out there and upset somebody. Australia and the Soviet Union had the teams to beat in that race, but we didn't care about them at all. What concerned us was giving it the very best we possibly could on that afternoon.

There were six countries in that relay race. Mae Faggs started it off for us and got a good start. She came around about even in front and handed it off to Margaret Mathews. Margaret ran a decent leg, then passed it to me. It was a clean pass, and I got off well. I think I passed two people on my leg, then handed it to Isabelle Daniels, who ran anchor. She ran a fine leg and just missed getting us into second place. But we had a strong and clean third-place finish, and we also had bronze medals for ourselves and for the United States. Not many people at the games expected us to do as well as we did, and that added to our happiness.

We had proved the experts wrong. All four of us squeezed onto the victory stand, and all four of us got bronze medals draped around our necks. Then they played the Australian national anthem—the Australian girls won the race—and I remember standing there, thinking to myself, "Be happy that you've got something to take back to Tennessee, and be happy that you're coming back with a bronze medal instead of just being eliminated from the 200 meters." I was happy that I salvaged something out of Melbourne, and a bronze medal still isn't all that bad for a high school kid from Tennessee.

I was disappointed, yes, but on the other hand, I wasn't disappointed. I had mixed feelings after I was through in Melbourne. I was disappointed in not qualifying for the 200, and I was disappointed that Coach Temple wasn't there to help us out when we needed it most. But on the other hand, how could I be disappointed in the whole experience itself? The travel, the glamour, the excitement that goes with being a part of an Olympic team. Besides, I had really accomplished a part of what I had set out to do—not the whole thing, but a part of it, anyway. I had won a medal, and I also had a goal to take home along with it, a goal to come back someday and win some more, gold ones. The games went on for another week after we were finished. All I did was watch. Bobby Morrow was the star of the United States' men's track team that year, and he cleaned up for us.

Just before the games ended, I noticed that everybody started to feel sad, like a very nice thing was coming to a close. Some of the girls actually cried, knowing that the end was near and that we'd all have to go home. All of us made so many friends we didn't want to leave behind; we did the next best thing to staying—we gave them a little of ourselves and they gave us a little of themselves. The exchanging of gifts that was going on was incredible. We all exchanged our sweatsuits, shirts, souvenirs of all kind. Some of the girls especially liked the bright-colored uniforms that some countries wore, and everybody wanted an American uniform. After the closing ceremonies, I still did not know that the 1960 Olympics were going to be held in Rome, Italy, but I did have this feeling that wherever they were held, I was going to be in them.

The trip home was a lot different from the trip over. For one thing, the sense of expectation was gone, and everybody was genuinely in a hurry to get back to the United States. I was because I knew the Olympics had stretched into November, and back home in Clarksville, November meant the basketball season. We stopped at the Fiji Islands for fuel, in Hawaii again, and then landed in Los Angeles. I flew on to Nashville the next day and, when I got home to Clarksville, Coach Temple was there waiting for me.

He told me that the Burt High School had been closed down for the day so all the kids could go to a special assembly in honor of me. When I got there, all the kids were excited and cheering; they gave me flowers, and the principal got up and made a speech, and then he called on me to come up and make a speech, too. That scared me more than the Olympics had. But all I did was get up there to the microphone and tell everybody how great it was to be back home in Clarksville and how much I had to share with all of them. It was a tremendous experience, one I'll never forget.

When the assembly finally ended, I left the auditorium and chased down after the basketball coach, Clinton Gray. When I finally found him, I said, "Coach, this is Friday night, and I hear the first basketball game of the season is going to be played tonight. Is that right?"

"Yes, Wilma," he said, "that's right."

So I said, "Look coach, I been away at the Olympics and all, and I been doing more running than basketball playing, but I'll tell you something, Coach Gray. I am in great shape." He smiled. Then I asked him, "Coach, can I play tonight? Please?"

He smiled again. Then he said, "Yes."

# 9

## Becoming a Woman

That basketball season, my junior year in high school, we had one of the best teams in the history of Tennessee. We didn't lose a game that season, and we were the first girls' team in the state to start scoring over 100 points a game. I averaged 35 points a game myself, and Nancy Bowen did even better than that, around 38. We made it to the state tournament again; this time it was played in the gym at Tennessee State over in Nashville. We played Merry High School from Jackson, Tennessee, in the final game; that was the school where my basketball coach, Clinton Gray, was from. He was really emotional about that game, he wanted to win it so badly, and all of us wanted to win it for him. We did, but it was close. I got 25 points that night, and we won by two or three, but I was disappointed in myself because I thought I could do better than that.

I always felt that people expected me to do better than that, because I had been on the Olympic team and all. I put a lot of pressure on myself, I guess, and I spent a lot of time looking over my shoulder, wondering if people were saying bad things about me, and feeling that a lot of them would be happy if I failed. During that state tournament, I was very sick as well. My tonsils were acting up, my throat was sore, and I remember I had trouble eating for a whole week. I couldn't swallow, my throat was always sore, and I couldn't even say more than two or three words at a time. In a regular game, I would be open for a shot in the corner, say, and when that usually happened, I'd scream for the ball. In that championship game, I had to clap my hands instead whenever I was open, and people were missing me.

But something happened after that game that hurt me very deeply and took away some from the joy of winning that state championship. We were in the closing seconds of the game; we were ahead by a couple of points, and I had the ball. We were supposed to hold onto the ball, keep the other team from getting it, the standard last-second freeze. Well, I threw the ball away. Since I had it last, and since it got away, I was responsible. Luckily, the Merry team couldn't capitalize on it; the clock ran out before they got a chance to shoot. Pandemonium broke loose, kids were all over the court, cheering and feeling really happy. Suddenly, Coach Gray, who was near the bench, started screaming at me. He said something like, "That was a stupid thing to do, throw the ball away like that. How can you be so stupid?" He really yelled, right in front of everybody, the game was over and everything and we had already won. Everybody heard him yelling at me, and the cheering stopped, and it became kind of quiet in the gym. It was like he threw a blanket on the whole celebration.

Well, I just went over to the bench, snatched up my jacket, and walked in a hurry to the locker room. A couple of the other girls came in, and I unloaded. I started telling them, "What's wrong with that man? Why'd he scream and yell at me like that? I hate him. He makes me sick. Why's he always trying to make an example out of me by picking on me all the time?"

I didn't know Coach Gray was right behind the wall, hearing everything. When I saw him, he had tears in his eyes, and he started walking back outside the locker room. I ran after him, and I caught up with him in the hall. I told him I was sorry but that I was upset that he screamed and yelled at me like that in front of everybody. Then I started to cry, and the two of us just stood there in the hallway, crying. Finally, we hugged and made up.

He took us out to dinner after the game, the whole team, but there was a tension in the air that shouldn't have been on the night you win a state championship. That was one thing about playing for Coach Gray. There always seemed to be this mixture of love and friction and conflict on the team, something I couldn't come to terms with. To this day, I think, "We just won the state tournament, and there he is in the middle of the victory celebration, screaming and yelling at me. Why?"

After the state tournament, I went right back into track, and it was a little different. For one thing, I was feeling that since I had been to the Olympics, everybody was expecting me to be nothing but phenomenal all the time. I had already picked up a lot of little snide remarks during the basketball season, kids saying, "Hey, she's no better than we are, she ain't so hot"—things like that. They either put you on a pedestal, or else they put you down. There was no in-between. It was the same with my own peer group at school; all the kids acted differently toward me after I came back from Melbourne. I was starting to feel that it was difficult to go out in the world and accomplish something, and then come back and be friends with everybody again. It isn't that easy. When you go and do something, they sometimes make you feel like an outcast when you get back.

Anyway, in track that season, we had the same kind of schedule we always had, a lot of playday-type meets and things, but I noticed that a lot of girls were dropping out rather than run against me. Here I was a little afraid, saying to myself, "Now look, you been to the Olympics and you can't let yourself lose to any of these high school kids." But they were saying to themselves, "Oh no, I'm not running against her; she's been to the Olympics, and I don't have a chance." So they dropped out. What they did was make it easy for me, and I won everything that year.

The school year ended with the Junior-Senior Prom, and it turned out to be my first experience with tragedy. I had waited for years to go to a prom, and Robert was going to be my escort. We both used to talk about going to a prom together, how much fun it would be to dress up in formal wear ourselves after watching all the older kids do it for years. I remember I had a blue evening dress, and Robert gave me a white orchid to wear with it. My parents couldn't afford to buy me a prom dress, but I got lucky because I knew Shirley Crowder who ran track at Tennessee State, and she told me she would let me borrow her blue dress for the prom. So I took her up on it, and it was really beautiful. Robert borrowed his daddy's brand-new car—a two-tone blue Ford—and we showed up at the high school gym in fine style.

By this time, Robert was the star of the school's football and basketball team, and I was the star of track and girl's basketball; we were like the King and Queen. The prom was nice, although kids will be kids. A lot of the boys snuck into the boys' room, or the locker room, and they drank Thunderbird wine, and a lot of the girls snuck into the girls' room and shared cigarettes. I walked into the girls' room; the windows were wide open, and the smoke was so thick you couldn't even breathe. I remember asking one of the girls to let me try smoking a cigarette, and everybody said, "No, no, Coach Gray will kill us if you ever do." But I persisted; this was prom night, you know, and anything goes. So they finally passed me a cigarette—an unfiltered cigarette—and I didn't know what I was doing with it. They gave it to me near the end, and I took a puff, and I got the end wet. Since cigarettes were scarce, and since I just ruined one by wetting the end, they cut me off. No more cigarettes for Wilma. They had a good excuse.

I had already made plans to spend the prom night at the house of my old friend Delma. After the prom, all of us decided to go up to Hopkinsville, Kentucky, about twenty-five miles away, to this club where we could be served some drinks without anybody asking any questions. Like kids, we all went out the door, and everybody said, "Last one to Hopkinsville is a chicken." Everybody jumped into cars and raced like hell, speeding all the way. Naturally, Robert and I were the first ones there, and we all stayed in this club for about an hour. About one o'clock in the morning, a fight broke out in the place, and people were throwing chairs and bottles and tables, everything. So Robert grabbed me, and said, "Let's get out of here," and all the other kids from Clarksville followed us out.

Again, we baited each other. "Last one back to Clarksville is a chicken." Robert and I got a head start on everybody else, and we got back home way before anybody else did. We drove straight over to Delma's house and sat out front for a while; then we went inside. We finally fell asleep around three in the morning, never giving a thought to something bad happening. But something terrible did.

Nancy Bowen, the basketball star who always outscored me, was killed, along with this boy, on the way back to Clarksville. Nancy didn't have a date that night, and neither did the boy she was in the car with. When everybody left the place where the fight broke out, she jumped into this classmate's car along with three other people. The boy had just finished driver's education and had gotten his license. On the way back from Kentucky, he was drag-racing with this other kid; he was doing about ninety miles an hour, and he lost control of the car. It went head-first into one of the pillars underneath a bridge, head-first into a concrete pillar at ninety miles an hour. He and Nancy were killed instantly. The car was demolished, and the three other kids in the car with them were seriously injured.

Around four in the morning, the telephone rang at Delma's house. Delma's mother answered it. It was Coach Gray, crying and hysterical on the other end. He said, "Is Wilma there? Is Delma there?" When she said yes, he said, "Thank God, let me talk with them."

She woke me up, and I took the phone. Coach Gray said, "Wilma ... Wilma ... is that really you?"

I said "Yes, what's wrong? You sound terrible."

He kept saying, "Thank God you're alive, thank God." Then he broke the news to me—"Nancy Bowen is dead." He said he thought she was riding with Robert and me. She would have been, too, had she had a date. But since she didn't, she didn't want to ride with people coupled off.

I couldn't believe my ears. Nancy and I had been close friends for years; she loved basketball as much as I did, and there were many days when we'd be inside that gym, playing basketball, practicing, when the other girls were thinking about everything else but basketball. That's how close we were. Now she was dead. At sixteen. I couldn't believe it.

Nancy's death was my first experience with tragedy. I couldn't handle it. I was an emotional wreck for weeks. I couldn't even think about that prom night without thinking about that telephone call in the middle of the night, and I'd fall apart again. I went back to Tennessee State that summer for more track under Coach Temple. He knew I was having trouble concentrating because that accident was always in the back of my mind. He knew Nancy and had refereed in many basketball games she played in, and he knew what my problem was. But he also knew that only time could heal a wound such as that. Slowly, I started coming out of it; being in another city, in another atmosphere, helped me do it. But to this day, I hear the word "prom" and feel bad.

That fall, I began my senior year in high school. That fall, I also realized that I was in love with Robert. We had been liking each other ever since the first grade in school, and now it was becoming something else. I was wearing his football jacket when the senior year at school started. He was a big star in both football and basketball, and we were the top couple in the school. I started liking him way back when; he was always so neat and clean when he came to school, he always dressed better than anybody else, and he wore these cute glasses. He was spoiled rotten; his mother doted on him and always picked him up from school. She was a hairdresser, and when

Robert and I started going together that fall, she would always do my hair for free.

He had this devilish streak in him, always in some kind of trouble. He used to pass by my house when I was little, and I'd point him out to my mother, sitting on the front porch, and I'd say, "Mother, that's Robert, and he's the boy I like." Robert was actually the only boy I had ever gone out with during all of those years; I didn't have time to meet a lot of boys because of track and because I really didn't have the desire to meet a lot of other boys since I liked Robert so much. What did I need to know all these other boys for?

When the basketball season started my senior year, I went to the doctor, Dr. Coleman, for my annual preseason physical exam. When it was over, he said to me, "Wilma, I want you to come back in a couple of days, I want to talk with you privately." When I went back to see him, he said, "Wilma, I have some news for you. You are pregnant." He said the baby was due in the summer, and the first thing I should do was have a talk with my mother and my father. He assured me he wouldn't tell a soul, not even my coach.

I was mortified. Pregnant? I couldn't understand it. Robert and I had just started to get involved in sex, and here I was pregnant. We were both innocent about sex, didn't know anything about birth control or about contraceptives, but neither one of us ever thought it would result in this. Pregnant. I refused to tell a soul. Telling my mother and father was out; I couldn't even face the thought of telling them, because I knew they would be crushed. I wasn't going to tell the coach a word, either, because that would be the end of my basketball career. I thought about Coach Temple, and about the Olympics, and track, and I couldn't bear to think about what the news would do to him, so high were his expectations for me. So I just kept the secret to myself and didn't tell anybody for weeks.

One day, Coach Gray started getting on me during basketball practice. "What's wrong with you, Wilma? You're getting lazy out there, not running after the ball, and you're getting kinda fat." So he went over to see Dr. Coleman, and he asked Dr. Coleman if anything strange had turned up during my preseason physical examination. Dr. Coleman, bless his heart, told the coach, "Well, since you asked, I think Wilma may be working on a tumor in her stomach." He never did come right out and say that I was pregnant.

Coach Gray came back and called me into his office. He said, "I just saw the doctor, and I know he's covering for you. You're pregnant, Wilma, and it's serious. You're going to have a baby, and you need to talk to your parents about this. This is more important than basketball." But going to my parents with the news was still out as far as I was concerned. I knew it would crush my mother, and my father, well, I was the apple of his eye, and the news would probably kill him.

So I finally decided to talk with my older sister, Yvonne. I told her I was around four or five months pregnant. She asked me if I had told Mother and Father? I said no. But I did notice

110

that my mother had started giving me suspicious looks, like she already knew something was happening. She had a lot of kids herself. Robert, meanwhile, had just started dating this other girl, and that really destroyed me, because I felt that now he was deserting me just as my whole world was about to collapse. So my sister Yvonne said, "I'll break the news to Mother," and she did. My father found out from my mother. My mother's reaction was great. She said she'd stick with me, no matter what. My father said two things. "One, no more Robert; I forbid you to see him again. Two, don't worry about anything, don't be ashamed of anything, everybody makes mistakes."

But the news was soon out on the grapevine, and one day Coach Temple showed up at my house. He sat down with me and my mother and father, and said he had come over from Nashville because he had just heard some startling news. He said he heard I was pregnant. We all nodded. Then I went and hid. I couldn't face him. When I finally came out of hiding, he said, "Wilma, I still want you to come to Tennessee State after the baby is born." I was overjoyed when he said that, because I already knew that Coach Temple had a standing rule than he never took a girl into his track program who had a baby. So he was breaking one of his own rules for me, and that made me feel absolutely great. The people I loved were sticking by me, and that alone took a lot of pressure, and pain, and guilt, off my shoulders.

The basketball season ended abruptly for me

that season, and the track season was out. I was at the height of my pregnancy during the track season and never did get to run a single stride that season, which should have been my best since I was a senior. At the end of May, 1958, I was graduated from high school; I was seven months pregnant. I went up there and took all of the honors, just like everybody else.

In those days, abortions were unheard-of, and nobody was sent away to live with an aunt for a while like the white girls did. The black girls stayed in school pregnant, like nothing was wrong at all. There were lots of other girls in that school in the same condition that I was in, and there really wasn't any stigma to it at all. The only stigma I felt was that people could gossip about me because they knew the real reason I wasn't running track that spring. My only concern after graduation was having a healthy baby and then getting myself back into shape for track. The scholarship was waiting for me at Tennessee State in September, and all I had to do was give birth and then start running on my own to get back in shape.

In July, I had a baby girl at the hospital in Clarksville. I named her Yolanda.

# 10

## The Road to Rome

I entered Tennessee State as a freshman six weeks later. At that time, September of 1958, my father had become very sick, and my mother was working to keep the family going. She didn't have time to take care of Yolanda. I certainly couldn't take care of her and be a freshman in college and a track star, too, so a unique arrangement was worked out. My sister Yvonne was married and living in St. Louis with her five-year-old son, Tony. Since Tony was old enough to go to nursery school, which meant that my mother could come home from work every day and still have time to go to the nursery school and pick up Tony and care for him at night, my mother, my sister Yvonne, and I worked out a plan. Since Yvonne wasn't working, she would have the time for a newborn baby, and since my mother could care for Tony, it was agreed that my mother would take Tony, and Yvonne would take my baby, Yolanda. So Tony came to Clarksville to live with my mother and go to nursery school there, my little baby went to St. Louis with

Yvonne, and I went to Nashville to start school at Tennessee State.

Robert, the father of my baby, wanted to get married and set up a household, but my father absolutely forbid that. He didn't ever want to see Robert because he blamed him for getting me into the position I was in. So marrying Robert was out. Besides, I really didn't want to become a housewife at such an early age, I knew I could still be a runner, and I wanted to be able to go to the Olympics in 1960. To have abandoned all of that, while knowing it was possible for my baby to be taken care of, would have killed me. So I just made the arrangements with my mother and my sister, put marriage out of my head, and went off to school.

Funny, but one night, just before I went away to college, little Yolanda was crying because of a wet diaper. I got up and turned the light on and started changing her. Right in the middle of it, I heard this rapping on the window. I was terrified. I thought it might be a thief or someone trying to break in. So I shut off the light in a hurry. Then I sort of peeked out the window to see what I could see. Who do you think was out there rapping on the window but Robert? So I turned on the light again, and I finished putting the diaper on the baby in a hurry. I knew my room was far enough away from my mother and father's room that nobody in there would hear anything. Then I picked up the baby, and I opened the window, and held up Yolanda for Robert to see.

It was the first time he saw his little daughter.

He was barred from the hospital on my father's orders, and he was barred from my house. But he told me he had been staking out my bedroom window, figuring the baby would wake up with a wet diaper sometime during the night, and that I'd have to get up and change it. He said when he saw the light go on, he knew it was time to make his move. Robert wasn't trying to dodge any responsibility; it's just that my father took it out on him. Robert's mother, in fact, offered to pay one half of my hospital bills, but my father refused the offer. He paid the whole thing himself.

I ran well at Tennessee State that fall, and as Christmas time got near, I was starting to feel comfortable there. But at Tennessee State, we didn't have holiday vacations like the other kids had; the track people had to stay at school and practice. That meant we spent Christmas Eve in the dormitory, wishing each other Merry Christmas and feeling absolutely lousy. We ran every day during Christmas week. We were all a little depressed, and I think Coach Temple noticed that, so he decided to give all of us three days off between Christmas and New Year's. I was happy about that, but then I got to thinking, "Gee, I'd love to see my little baby up in St. Louis," but three days weren't enough to get back an and forth. So I went to Coach Temple, and I asked him for a couple more days off, and told him that I wanted to see my baby in St. Louis. "She's five months old now and I haven't seen her since back in September." Coach Temple said absolutely not; he said he was going to treat me just like every-

115

body else, three days off and that's it, no special favors. I accepted that, since I knew I was lucky to be there in the first place, having had a baby and all.

So I went back to Clarksville to begin those three days off. My sister Yvonne came over, and she said the baby was back in St. Louis with her friend. She also said, "Wilma, I've become very attached to that little baby, and I want to talk with you about the possibility of adopting the baby, since you're still in school and since I've got the time to take care of her and all." Well, I absolutely panicked. I never expected that; I never thought that my sister would want to keep my baby. I spent the rest of the day in a frenzy, thinking of ways of getting my baby back. I didn't have any money, and I knew my father wouldn't give me any. With no money, there's no way I could even get to St. Louis. So I went out into the streets of Clarksville, looking for Robert. I found him, and told him what was going on, and we sat down and talked and worked out a plan to get to St. Louis and steal our baby back.

Robert said, "Don't worry about transportation, I'll get my father's car. Don't worry about money, I'll get some of that, too. What we got to worry about is your father." So I went right back home, and I started going to work on my father. I begged and pleaded with him, and even made a deal with one of my older brothers, Roosevelt, that he would go with us as sort of a chaperon. I told my father, "What could go wrong, with Roosevelt right there?"

After hours of begging and crying, my father finally agreed that I could go with Robert to St. Louis and see my baby—but only if Roosevelt stayed with us at all times. I went right back to see Robert, told him the plan, and we talked about the whole thing some more. Then we smoothed out the plan one more time. Neither one of us wanted Roosevelt along, really, so we worked on a way to cut him out of the trip. We figured we'd wait until real late at night, when everybody—my father and Roosevelt included, was sound asleep, and then we'd go.

That's exactly what we did. I tiptoed back into my house about three in the morning, packed a little diaper bag, and then tiptoed out again and jumped into Robert's father's car, and off we went to St. Louis. We drove all night, got to St. Louis, to my sister's house, and snatched up the baby and left. We headed right back, and then Robert's father's car broke down. He had to call his father to bring another car, and we sat on the highway for most of the day waiting. The baby meanwhile was grinning and cooing and laughing; Robert and I both laughed because we knew that my father would be steaming mad by then, knowing I had taken off with Robert and left my brother Roosevelt behind.

When I finally did get home, my father sure enough was furious, but when he laid eyes on the baby, he calmed right down. In fact, after he played with the baby for a bit, he finally announced, "This baby ain't going nowhere. It's staying right here." Yolanda did stay right there, and my mother watched over her and took care of her like she was her own child. Robert's mother helped out, too, taking the baby to her house whenever she could. But getting my baby back made that little three-day vacation the wildest I've ever had. Before I knew it, I had to be back on campus. I just made it. I had some pictures of Yolanda with me for the other girls in the dorm to see. It's funny, but they all seemed to envy me that baby.

When I finally did have to bear down in school after the holidays, it really got tough. I was a freshman and that was a hard adjustment for me. I was running track, and that took up a lot of my time. I had to keep a two-point average in the classroom to keep my scholarship and stay in school, and that meant I had to study. I was majoring in elementary education, minoring in psychology. I was also a mother, and I wondered a lot how my baby was doing back home. Robert was dropping hints that I should drop out of school, quit track, and become a full-time wife and mother. It was tempting at times, I admit it. There were millions of times I just wanted to quit school and take the easy way out.

Once, when I was really brooding over it, wondering what to do, one of my teachers, his name was Mr. Knight, noticed that something was troubling me and he called me over and asked me to sit down and talk with him. I spilled it all out on him, how I was torn between this and that, and he talked with me like a father. He said he understood my situation, but he wanted me to think about two things. First, the baby was in good hands and was safe. The same person who raised me was now raising Yolanda. Second, he told me to think about all the sacrifices I had already made as far as track was concerned, and to ask myself if I really wanted to throw all of that away? He said, "Wilma, you *can* have both." I knew he was right, and I listened to him. But that night, I went back to my room in the dorm, and I closed the door, and I just lay on the bed and cried and cried. Nobody will ever know about that. But I decided to stay and stick it out.

By the time my sophomore year began, things started falling in place nicely. Yolanda was doing fine with my family back in Clarksville, my grades were holding, and I was running well. In fact, I was running better than ever. My speed was tremendous after I had the baby; I was much faster than before. At the end of my sophomore season, the Olympic Trials were scheduled, and that was what I had been waiting for. I wanted the Olympic Games badly. Almost four years had passed since Melbourne, and I had gone from a skinny little high school girl to a woman, a mother, a college student. The first real stop on the road to Rome that year was the National AAU meet in Corpus Christi, Texas. The best women there would be invited to the Olympic Trials a couple weeks later at Texas Christian University.

I remember the Nationals at Corpus Christi for two reasons. First, my little sister Charlene, the baby in the family, was invited by Coach Temple to run in the juniors, and she got sick. I watched over her the way people watched over me in 1956. She had a boil that actually made her ill, and had to be lanced. But she was all right after that. Second, I remember this incident in Corpus Christi. All of us were on this bus, all the kids who were at the AAU meet, white kids and black kids on the same bus. Well, the bus driver walked off and refused to drive the bus. They had to get another bus driver to take us around. The new driver didn't seem to like it very much either, having to drive an integrated bus, but he did it anyway.

I ran well in the Nationals, and I knew I was ready for some good times in the Olympic Trials. But I wasn't ready for what would happen as a result. What happened was that I ran a :22.9 in the 200 meters, the fastest 200 meters ever run by a woman. It was a world's record. But the AAU, and whoever else is in charge of validating world's records, took a whole damn year to make it official. As a result, you look in record books today and sometimes it isn't even mentioned. That :22.9 stood for almost eight years.

I remember the race like it was yesterday. I was with Vivian Brown, who was a very strong runner, one who would really make you work in a race. We talked before the start, and neither one of us seemed very psyched up about running that day. In fact, I remember Vivian saying to me, "God, I don't feel it in my bones today," and I remember saying back to her, "You're right, I don't feel much like running today myself." There was none of the usual pre-race tension and nervousness. We both were out there with the attitude, "Let's give it a shot, give it a run, and get it over with." It turned out to be the best race of my life at that point. A world's record, fastest time in the event ever run by a woman.

I remember when the race was over, I plopped down next to Coach Temple, and he was just smiling, and he said, "Doin' all right, aren't you?" That meant, "Good race, Wilma." I never knew I set a world's record, and he didn't tell me. I found out later when one of the other girls on the team came running over and said, "Why ain'tcha celebrating?"

I said, "Gee, I made the team, but I made the team once before, you know."

"No, that's not what I mean," she said. "I'm talking about the :22.9. It's a world record, you know."

I said, "It is?"

"You mean nobody told you?"

I said no. Then I said, "Well, let's you and me be off and get the celebrating started."

I actually made the Olympic team in 1960 in three events—the 100, 200, and relay. We trained that year at Kansas State University in Emporia, Kansas, but just before leaving Texas we learned that the coach of the United States Olympic team was going to be none other than Ed Temple, my coach at Tennessee State. Boy, was I overjoyed to hear that—how lucky can a girl get? My own coach, the one who stuck with me through thick and thin, was going to be the Olympic coach. I became very excited and knew that somebody up there was taking care of me this time around.

The facilities at Emporia, Kansas, were absolutely great; the living quarters were excellent, the track was fast, the people there were fabulous to us. One of the coaches at the school had this cabin right on a lake, and he took us there after practice; we swam and he fed us the biggest steaks I had ever seen, even bigger than the ones I had in Texas.

Even so, Coach Temple wasn't letting us get away with anything. He was running us three times a day, and he was making this Olympic practice a lot harder than the one I had been to in 1956. The girls on the team really didn't get to know each other until the day we all weighed in, that's how busy Coach Temple kept us. I weighed in at 129, and the weight for my height was supposed to be 140. No matter. Coach Temple knew I was running well. After a week, he cut me down to two practices a day, and after two weeks he trimmed it to one practice a day. He knew his runners like a book, and he didn't want me burning myself out before we got to Rome. I remember the people in that town made things so nice for us at night; they even opened the movie theaters for us and let us all in free.

The only problem we had those three weeks concerned riding bikes. There were bikes all over the campus for us to use, to get from place to place. But Coach Temple told us right off, "No bike riding at any time." He didn't want us using running muscles on anything else but running. So one day, we were all sitting around, and we were kinda bored, and all of these bikes were just sitting there, inviting us to ride them. So somebody got the bright idea, "What the hell, let's go ride them bikes." We all took off, and what happens? We get lost. We wind up in the woods someplace, and we have to pump those bikes for a couple hours just to find our way back. We got back to practice late, the muscles in the legs were sore, we were all tired out, and Coach Temple was furious. We all did some extra running that day as punishment, and we all collapsed into bed that night exhausted. The next morning, we had to help each other out of bed, that's how sore we all were.

But Coach Temple paid attention to details. Any of the girls who happened to have big breasts was outfitted with a special uplift bra; this was to keep them in place while they ran. He had this theory that women could damage themselves running unless their breasts were properly secured. His wife used to take the girls who needed these special bras to buy them, and she always made sure they were fitted properly. Another thing Coach Temple understood was the problem some girls had with menstruation. With some girls, stomach pains and cramps would really hamper their running, not to mention how uncomfortable it was running with sanitary pads. He took this into account during practices, and even during meets. The rest of us, meanwhile, would sit there with the dates of upcoming meets and try to figure out if the menstrual period would coincide with the track meet. If it did, we'd all moan and groan and curse a little, then psyche ourselves up, knowing that it was going to be a little bit tougher with it than without it, but that we'd have to run anyway. No matter what anybody says, running a race in the middle of a menstrual period is not easy.

Anyway, Coach Temple worked us very hard, but fairly, during that three-week training session in Kansas. Just having him there put me in an incredible frame of mind. I knew I was ready for the Olympics as a runner, no question about that. But I also knew I would be ready mentally no matter what, simply because he was the coach. It was like bringing your second father along to keep you up.

By the time that training camp broke, I knew there was a good chance to win three gold medals in Rome, and I knew if I didn't win three, it would be my fault alone. Everything was in place for me, and all I had to do was deliver my end of it. Coach Temple purposely avoided telling any of us about who the best competition was going to come from, but the rumors persisted anyway. Betty Cuthbert was coming back for one more try, and everybody was saying she was too old to win again. There were rumors about this beautiful, tall blond girl from Germany who was wiping out everybody in Europe. One day, somebody said to me, "Wilma, that blonde from Germany, she's as tall as you are." That worried me at first, because I had always had trouble running against girls who were tall and who had strides as long as mine. Then I said to myself, "Wait a minute, what am I doing worrying about her? She should be worrying about me because I'm the one who just got a world's record, that's why. Who's she, anyway?"

In that frame of mind, I went off to Rome.

## 11

# Rome

We spent a week in New York City before leaving for Rome, and during that week we were measured and outfitted with all of our Olympic uniforms and equipment. The women's track team left on an airplane with the men's rowing team, and we all arrived about two weeks before the games began. My first impression of Rome was that it was a storybook city come true: seeing the Coliseum, the catacombs, the Vatican, was like seeing pictures come to life. When we settled into the Olympic Village, Lucinda Williams was assigned as my roommate and, as things turned out, that was a very fortunate break for me.

The Olympic Village itself was smaller than the one in Melbourne, more compact, and the security was pretty loose; no armed guards or anything like that. The Italian people were very enthusiastic about having the Olympics in their country, and they seemed to be around all the time, in the dining halls, in the Village, talking with us, laughing. They were just the opposite of the Australians, who seemed reserved and detached about the

1956 games. The atmosphere in the village was more fun, too. We could eat anytime we wanted to eat, there was a recreation hall which everybody hung around in, and every night there was a dance. Since all the athletes from other countries wanted to learn the latest American dance steps, we were all in popular demand. We gave them the latest steps we learned straight from "American Bandstand" on television back home. They all thought we were the coolest cats.

We started practicing in the afternoons as soon as we got there, because Coach Temple was all business by now. The Italian language was giving us all a lot of problems, and the U.S. Olympic Committee gave us these little books, Italian-American dictionaries, and all of us walked around Rome with them. Sometimes, when we wanted to say something to an Italian, we would just point to the right phrase. Other times, we'd have to block out almost the whole page with our hands and leave one sentence, or one paragraph showing. Eventually, we started learning key phrases ourselves, but I think the Italian people got a kick out of us. They always laughed, and seemed so jolly.

Myself, I felt loose and free, and the reason was probably because Coach Temple was there. He meant that much to me. That whole first week, we worked out under various Italian starters, who issued commands in Italian, and we had to get used to that. Then, on the last day, the man who would be the actual starter in the games came by and we went through it all with him. I listened and got the commands down pat; I wasn't going to rely solely on the sound of the gun anymore. Otherwise, the first week in Rome was pleasant and uneventful. But it would heat up.

One day, Coach Temple sat me down, and we had a very serious talk. He said that he thought my chances were very good for winning three gold medals, and then he told me about this dream he had been having. He said that for two and three nights in a row, he had dreamt that I actually did it, won three gold medals and became the first American woman in Olympic history to have done that. I felt good about that, because I knew I was running well. My practice runs were great, and the weather in Rome was perfect for me—the temperatures were in the 100s, and it felt just like it felt down in Tennessee, where I had been running in the hot weather for years. My body was used to the heat, and the hot weather actually helped put me in a good frame of mind.

Early in the second week, the week before the games began, I had my first little emotional crisis. This track newsletter, which was published by Lord knows who, was circulating around, and it claimed to have the fastest times run by all the women at the Olympics. I found out that my name didn't appear until the sixth page. "The sixth page?" I said to myself. "What about the world's record I just set?" I was upset by that, and being on the sixth page upset me emotionally. Coach Temple said, "Don't worry about it, the newsletter doesn't mean anything; whoever put it together doesn't know anything." He said to me,

"You're running a consistent :11.4 in the 100, and there's nobody else here who can come close to that." That was the value of having him there; another coach wouldn't have known I was upset, and probably wouldn't have taken the time to boost my spirits when I needed them boosted. Coach Temple knew exactly what to do, always.

So finally it was Wednesday, the day before I was scheduled to run in my first race at Rome. Disaster. It was very hot that day, and we decided not to go to our assigned track to practice, since Coach Temple didn't want us to do anything more than jog a little, break a sweat, and walk out the kinks. So we went to this field right behind the Olympic Stadium; it was huge and just covered with nice green grass. The sprinklers were on, and the temperature was in the 100s again, and all of us started running through the sprinklers to cool off a little. It was great fun, an unexpected bonus for us. Time and again, we ran through the sprinklers, jumped through the spray, and got our uniforms and ourselves soaking wet. Right near the end of the session, I jumped over this sprinkler one last time—I never even saw the hole right behind it. Well, I stepped right into the hole, turned my ankle, and heard it pop.

Everybody came running over and they pulled it out, and I was crying because the ankle hurt very badly and I thought that I had broken it and that everything was down the drain now. The trainer took one look and made this horrible face; the ankle was swollen and already it was discolored. He immediately ordered some ice, and he packed it and they carried me back to my room. There, the trainer taped it up real tight, and my foot was elevated into the air. I stayed that way until the next morning. When I got up, I didn't know what to expect. I was due to run in the afternoon in the Olympics, and here I was with a sore and swollen ankle. When I got up, I put my weight on it and, thank God, it held. I said to myself, "Thank God, it's only a sprain, I can handle that because I don't have to run any curves today, just the straightaway in the 100."

Meanwhile, at the games rumors were flying around that I had broken my ankle and wouldn't be able to run. But nobody outside really knew what was going on. I knew I could run, and since I was going to be running the 100, I knew the ankle wouldn't hamper me that badly. Coach Temple sat with me on the bus ride to the Olympic Stadium, and he kept reassuring me that everything was going to be all right, and that is exactly what I needed to hear at the time.

When we got to the stadium, they lined us up right away in the order in which we were going to run, and then they put us through the tunnel which leads to the stadium. Coach Temple couldn't go through the tunnel, so we said goodbye there at the entrance, and I went into the tunnel alone. When I got into the tunnel with the other runners, a strange calm came over me. I was nervous in a sense, yes; but I also got a chance to take a look at the runners I would be going up against, and I felt, deep inside, that I could beat any of them. So I lay down on a bench and propped my feet up against the wall; I just lay there the whole time, waiting for them to call my name. When they did, I slowly got up and walked out into the Olympic Stadium for the first time as a participant.

The stadium was jammed; at least 80,000 people were inside it. For some reason, the Italian fans took a liking to me the very first day I arrived, and when they saw me walk out toward the track, they started cheering wildly and started chanting, "Vil-ma ... Vil-ma ..." I was overwhelmed by that, didn't expect it in a million years. But I decided right away to block it out of my mind. I didn't want anything to interfere with my concentration, and I was thinking, "You start smiling and waving and listening to the cheering and chanting, you're going to forget all about the real reason you're here. To win." So I put it all out of my head, and I walked slowly over to the starting blocks and took one practice start. I wasn't paying any attention to the other runners who were jumping all around and running and wasting energy. I just stayed around the starting block and waited. When the race went off, I got a good start and won easily. In the second trial heat, the same thing happened. I got off good and won without any trouble. The trial heats were conducted to whittle down the field of runners for the final on Saturday. But winning two on the first day didn't assure me of anything. I still had two more trial heats to run the next day.

That next day, I followed the same procedure. My ankle wasn't bothering me, and I actually fell asleep for a little while on the practice field. I went to sit down and rest for a bit, and my nervous reaction was to fall asleep. I won the third trial heat that day, but the fourth was the memorable one. I won it in a time of 11 seconds flat and that was a new world's record. But I didn't get it; the International Olympic Committee disallowed it because the wind velocity at my back was more than 2.2 miles an hour, it said. Now, any runner alive knows that when you're out there on the track you aren't even aware that the wind is blowing, so how could a two-mile-an-hour wind help you any? But that's what was said, and the record was not made official. That meant I lost two world records in a matter of a month because the officials disallowed them.

Coach Temple and I were upset over the ruling, but we both decided to forget about it so it wouldn't be on my mind when I ran the finals on Saturday. But other people didn't forget. Coming off the field that day, I suddenly had a million microphones in my face, and the crowd never stopped chanting, "Vil-ma . . . Vil-ma . . ."

Saturday. This was the day. The final in the women's 100 meters. The top three people, out of six, were Jutta Heine, the tall blond girl from West Germany; Dorothy Hyman, from Great Britain, and myself. I really felt insecure about Jutta Heine all that morning. She had won all of her preliminary heats, just as I had, and she was just as tall as I was. I watched her run a heat and noticed that she had a stride just as long as I had, and, yes, she was a good runner. You knew immediately about those things; you can see it in the way runners carry themselves. But I guess I was the favorite going in; my times in the heats were :11.3 twice, and :11.4.

The tension began for all of us in the tunnel which leads out to the stadium. There was no way to get away from each other; you mingle, and you avoid looking, and you try to get yourself in a proper frame of mind. It's a little bit like a fighter before a big championship bout. Yes, you have to build up a little hatred for your opponents, and you have to psyche yourself up to instill the killer instinct. But I was not afraid or intimidated in that tunnel. I never talked, but I always looked the others straight in the eye. I knew that even if I did say something, they wouldn't be able to understand me anyway; the little English they did know would have been lost in my black southern accent. So I just kept quiet and looked them in the eyes. When we got out on the track, I followed my same routine: one practice start, then slowly walk around, with my hands on my hips, near the starting blocks. No rushing, no jumping, no running around; conserve the energy for when it really matters. I was concentrating deeply.

My start was relatively good. I came out second or third in the field, and my speed started increasing the farther I went. When I reached fifty meters, I saw that I had them all, and I was just beginning to turn it on. By seventy meters, I knew the race was mine, nobody was going to catch me. I won by five to seven yards, and Dorothy Hyman was second, and I knew then and there that Jutta

Heine would not beat me. I did 11 flat again, and this time there was another mixup involving one of the officials, and the world's record was discounted. I couldn't believe that. I cried, and my coach was upset, but I was happy that I had won my first gold medal easily.

When I got back to my room, the first telegram I received was from Betty Cuthbert, the Australian runner who had won three gold medals in 1956. She was going to try for three more in 1960, but she had gotten hurt and couldn't run at all. Soon, there were so many flowers and telegrams coming into my room that the place was overrun. A lot of them were coming in from back home in Clarksville, Tennessee, and they affected me the most.

There was also some humor, and humor was needed at a time like that. For example, there was a man at Tennessee State, my school, who was the official school photographer. His name was Earl Clanton III, and Coach Temple always called him "The Third." Well, the school figured we were going to do well at the Olympics so they sent "The Third" all the way over from Nashville to Rome to take exclusive pictures. So, newspapermen and photographers were pounding on the doors looking for interviews and pictures, and we held them all off so we could give "The Third" some exclusive shots. For a half hour, we stood around waiting for him, and then the international press finally stampeded in. For the next hour and a half, all I did was pose for pictures for the AP, the UPI, Italian papers, and answer every conceivable question. During these ninety minutes, a couple thousand pictures must have been taken. Finally, when all the newsmen and photographers started leaving, Coach Temple went over to Earl Clanton and said, "Hey, how'd ya do, Third?"

Earl Clanton swallowed a little bit, and then he said, "Coach, I didn't get nothin'. The camera's workin'."

The next morning, Sunday morning, I had breakfast with Coach Temple. He said to take it easy for as long as I could and, after the 200 meter race, I'd be free to do whatever I wanted in Rome. He told me to rest the ankle as long as I could because on Tuesday, in the 200-meter final, I'd be running curves for the first time since I had sprained it. Tuesday broke raining. It was miserable out there, but I felt good, no real pressure. The 200 was mine, I loved it more than anything else. A little rain meant nothing to me. In fact, before the start of the race, I was saying to myself, as a way of psyching up, "There's nobody alive who can beat you in the 200. Go get it."

The rain did slow me down a little, but I won the race easily, no problem with the ankle, no problem with the start. I really won that race a lot easier than I thought I would, against Jutta Heine and Dorothy Hyman and pretty much the same field that was in the 100. The time was 24 seconds flat, and that was like walking. I was disappointed, because I had been doing a consistent :22.9 in the 200, and 24 flat was embarrassing. Still, I said to myself that night, "That's two gold medals down and one to go."

On Friday, the 440 relay was scheduled. That was my chance to become the first American woman ever to win three Olympic gold medals. I wasn't about to blow it. The team was: Martha Hudson, running the first leg; Barbara Jones, running the second; Lucinda Williams, running the third, and me, running anchor. The teams everybody was talking about were Russia, West Germany, and Britain. Well, we wiped them all out, and we set a world's record in the process. This time, they gave us the record, no wind faults or official botch-ups. It was an easy race for us; everybody ran their best, and we won it going away.

When I broke the tape, I had my three gold medals, and the feeling of accomplishment welled up inside of me. The first American woman to win three Olympic gold medals. I knew that was something nobody could ever take away from me, ever. After the playing of "The Star-Spangled Banner," I came away from the victory stand and I was mobbed. People were jumping all over me, pushing microphones into my face, pounding my back. I couldn't believe it. Finally, the American officials grabbed me and escorted me to safety. One of them said, "Wilma, life will never be the same for you again." He was so right.

For one thing, I noticed that some animosity was developing toward me on the part of some other American women runners. There were whispers and rumors and some nasty things said about me getting all of the publicity and the attention and them not getting their share. That may have been so, but I certainly wasn't seeking out any publicity and, after all, I *did* win three gold medals.

But the good part was in meeting such people as Pope John XXIII. The whole American team was invited to the Vatican to meet him, and what I remember first about the Vatican was that everybody inside of it talked in whispers. So I started whispering, and so did the rest of the athletes. I was Protestant, Southern Baptist, and all I knew about the Pope was that he was the head of the Roman Catholic Church.

As it turned out, Pope John was a real jolly fellow; he had rosy cheeks and he laughed a lot. He was a very happy and vibrant man, and it was obvious that everybody around him loved him. He talked to us in a group, and he said that each and every one of us was a winner, and we all know that on one single day, only one of us will be able to win again. But his message was simple, and it was nice: you are all outstanding people, win or lose.

He was a lot different from Pope Paul VI, who I had met in a private audience a year or two later. Pope Paul had my family names memorized, the ages of my kids memorized, and he was very somber and cold. All the people around him were wearing these long black robes and were just as somber as he was. I felt uncomfortable and wanted to get out of there as soon as I could. But with Pope John I did feel very comfortable, very relaxed. When our session with him was over, he even gave each of us his own little blessing, and that was nice, too.

I desperately wanted to go back home to Tennessee after the Olympics ended, but no such luck. From Rome, Coach Temple took me and a couple other girls who had won medals to the British Empire Games in London. It was terrible. It rained the whole time we were there, and everything I had heard about London turned out to be true—it was dark and dreary, damp. The fog rolled in early, and when I looked at the street lights at night all I could think of was Jack the Ripper. Walking those streets in that weather you couldn't see ten feet in front of you. I won two events in the British Empire Games, the 100 and the relay. They were the only events Coach Temple entered me in; his theory was why try to recreate the Olympic triple everywhere else?

As it turned out, I never lost another race that year—and the animosity toward me was building up, even to the point where some of the girls from Tennessee State, girls I had been running with and living with for years, were turning on me. Lucinda Williams stuck with me like a true sister, but I was having my troubles with some of the others. A couple even stopped speaking to me. It all came to a head in London—literally. The incident that brought it out into the open went like this.

I had run that day in the rain, and my hair was a mess. There was a big banquet at night, and by the time I got back to my room I only had an hour or so to get ready. My sweat clothes were dripping wet and I was desperate for the hot hair curlers to set my hair. On the road, we all shared the same hot curlers to make it easier for traveling; the lighter your luggage is on such things as curlers, the more gifts you can get into it. Well, there I was running around the room, then from room to room, looking for the curlers, and the other girls were pretending they had no idea whatsoever where the curlers were. I was frantic. I didn't have the time to get my hair done, so I went to the banquet with my hair an absolute mess and Coach Temple blew his top. He called everybody in later, demanded an explanation, and everybody played stupid. But both he and I knew they had hidden the curlers on purpose to make me look bad in public. I was upset by this, too, but I let him handle it.

The next day, we had to run the relay race in the British Empire Games. The very same team that had just won an Olympic gold medal and set a world's record was running. Well, the other three girls decided they just weren't going to run that day, that they'd go out there and run maybe just as fast as it took for them to stay in the race, no faster. White Stadium in London was packed with people who wanted to see the fastest women's relay team in history, but these girls were going to dog it. The race began, and they barely struggled along. By the time I got the baton, on the anchor leg, one girl was actually forty yards ahead of me with only 110 yards to go. Well, I was determined to win that race, because sometime during the middle of it I realized what was really happening. So I poured it on like never before, ran the fastest anchor leg of my life, and caught up with her at the very tip of the tape to win. I closed the forty yards and actually pulled out the race, and the crowd went crazy.

I got a standing ovation. Although I was mad at the others because I felt they had betrayed me, still I felt kind of good because winning the way I did only made it worse for them. Coach Temple saw immediately what was going on, and after the race, he called them all in and chewed them out. "When we get back to Tennessee State," he told them, "all three of you are on probation." That left me with three angry teammates, and a whole lot of meets to go with them. That was not the very best situation in the world to be in, to put it mildly.

The next stop after London was Stuttgart, Germany, for an invitational meet featuring Olympic winners. It rained the whole time we were there, too—it was late fall in Europe. I did an :11.2 to win the 100 in Germany, then went to Holland and did an :11.1 to win there. We bounced around for three more weeks in Europe, traveling and competing in meets.

The girls were not speaking to me, and the situation with them was getting even worse. What was horrible was that we could not even bring it out into the open among ourselves; it was three against one. They were always talking around me whenever I was there, like I was a spy or something. Finally, to the relief of absolutely everyone, Coach Temple called us in and announced that we were going home, pack up.

What a joy: going home! I wanted so much to

be with my parents, my family, my friends. I hadn't seen them in almost two months, although I had received telegrams from them and I knew they had been watching the Olympics on television. I was so happy. I had come to Rome, accomplished what I had wanted to accomplish. I had three gold medals, and now I wanted to share them with the people I loved most. Coach Temple said the plan was to fly from Rome to New York City, then from New York to Nashville. From there, he said, we could drive the fifty miles to Clarksville. So began a strange and tiring journey and a lot of days in airplanes and airports.

When I finally got off the plane in Nashville, the first person I saw was Coach Temple's wife. Then I saw this monstrous crowd right behind her. Everybody was there, it seemed—mayors of cities, the governor, judges, television stations, marching bands from the Tennessee State campus. They had a tremendous reception for us all at the Nashville airport, and then Coach Temple said to me, "Come on, you've got to stay here for a couple of days before going home." I asked why? He said, "Because the people in Clarksville have this big celebration planned, and they didn't know when you were coming back, and now that they know you're back it's going to take them two days to put the big parade and things together." I felt terrible. After all those days on airplanes and in airports, I get so close to home and they put me in a holding pattern.

That night, when everybody thought I was sleeping in the dorm, I talked myself into a ride,

141

snuck back into Clarksville, and had a tearful and joyful private reunion with my mother and my father. I was back at Tennessee State the next morning to wake up as if nothing happened. That's running.

# 12

## Spoils to the Victor

The Clarksville parade for me actually began two miles outside the city, when the police escort picked us up on the highway and started leading us into town. Along the way, the motorcade was joined by a car that included some very important people—my mother and father, one of my older brothers and his wife, and my baby girl, Yolanda. As we got closer to Clarksville, I saw the crowd up ahead and I figured that all 40,000 people in the city had shown up.

As it turned out, this particular parade had a social significance far beyond the welcoming of Wilma Rudolph back home. Clarksville, at the time, was still a segregated city, and parade actually was the first integrated event in the history of the town. So was the banquet they gave for me that night; it was the first time in Clarksville's history that blacks and whites had gathered under the same roof for the same event. That's why it took so long to organize everything; the traditional all-white organizations were going to be represented in the parade, the American Legion, the VFW, the Elks. So were the traditional black groups, the black high school marching band, the black ministers, the various black fraternal organizations.

This parade broke the color barrier in Clarksville, and who was at the head of it but the white mayor of town. I was in an open convertible, standing and waving to everybody along the parade route. Everybody who meant anything in my life was there for that parade, my grade-school teachers, Coach Gray, everybody. Everybody, that is, except Robert, the boy I was in love with. He was up in Indiana, playing it cool, visiting relatives and staying out of sight.

We even had the United States Army in on the act. A whole group of soldiers from Fort Campbell, Kentucky, which is not far from Clarksville, marched in the parade and, after the parade was over, we all went over to Fort Campbell, where the generals were all waiting for us. They gave a parachute demonstration for us, and a little reception afterward. When that ended, I had about an hour left to go home, change clothes, and get over to the big banquet they were throwing in my honor at the Clarksville Armory.

I remember that banquet vividly because the armory was jammed with black people and white, and that had never happened before in Clarksville. I also remember vividly a speech that was made that night by this old white judge, Judge Hudson. He got up there that night, knowing exactly what was happening, and he said, "Ladies and gentlemen, you play a piano. You can play very nice music on a piano by playing only the black keys on it, and you can play very nice music on the same piano by playing only the white keys on it. But, ladies and gentlemen, the absolute best music comes out of that piano when you play both the black keys and the white keys together." Everybody applauded.

That was a historic day for the town, and certainly for me. But it was only the beginning. The next three or four days I was supposed to be resting, taking it easy for the first time in many months, reliving my Olympic experiences with my mother and father. But I never did get a chance to relax. People were coming over to my house in steady streams, friends, relatives, newspaper reporters wanting stories, photographers wanting pictures. I especially wanted to talk with my father, who was so proud of me. But he said, "Don't worry about me, you talk with the folks, that's all part of it for you."

Actually, the night of the banquet in my honor, my father took very ill—he was a diabetic—he collapsed right on the stage. But he refused to be taken home. He kept pushing everybody off, saying, "I'm all right, just leave me alone." He stayed to the very end that night, and he said the next day that the reason he stayed was because he didn't want to miss a single thing that was going on. He told me before the Olympics, "Don't you worry about me none. I'll be here when you get back. You just go and run." He died the following April.

The next stop on this homecoming celebration tour was Chicago. Mayor Daley greeted us, and he gave me the keys to the city. Then we went to Detroit for a banquet. We stayed in the very best hotels and ate in the best restaurants, Coach Temple and myself and a couple of other people, a chaperone for me, my mother most of the time. All of the events were lined up by the Tennessee State alumni, who seemed to be everywhere in America. I think I covered every state in the country that year on tour. In Atlanta, it was the 100 Per Cent Wrong Club, a group of black businessmen, who sponsored the banquet and gave me an award; in New York City, it was the NAACP, and Roy Wilkins was the speaker; in Philadelphia, I was presented at a cotillion ball, and in Washington, I met ambassadors of countries I never knew existed. It was one big social whirl, and I was getting spoiled rotten. I didn't even do my own hair; everywhere I went, somebody always did it for me, and it never cost me a cent.

I was winning awards, too. I won the Female Athlete of the Year award, and the Sullivan Award, which goes to the top amateur athlete in the United States. That was the one everybody wanted to win and I was proud of getting it. I got to meet and spend time with such people as Lena Horne and Harry Belafonte. Everybody was making decisions for me; I never had to think about anything else but looking pretty and smiling a lot. On the rare occasions that I got back to school, I picked up a job working for Coach Temple in the Tennessee State post office—he and his wife ran it. I made $62 a week as salary, and they gave me a laundry fee that sometimes went over $100 when I came back from the road. I pledged to the Delta Sigma Phete sorority on campus and my life was absolutely wonderful, except, of course, for the lingering animosity on the part of some of the girls I had run with. When the indoor season came around, I got myself into shape to run again, and I was off.

I was the first woman to be invited to run in such meets as the New York Athletic Club meet, the Millrose Games, the Los Angeles Times' Games, the Penn Relays, the Drake Relays. Up to that time, no women had ever run in those meets. I was the first, and the doors have been open ever since to women. I'm proud of that to this day. When they invited me, they always invited six or seven other girls to run against me. Indoors, I couldn't run my specialty events, the 100 and the 200. Indoors, the distances are shorter, and I had to settle on the 50, the 60, and the 70.

I was winning, even though I was still having trouble with the shorter distances because of my starts. I lost once indoors, and that was in Los Angeles; the papers the next day ran big headlines, WHAT'S WRONG WITH WILMA? Nothing was wrong. I just got beat that night, fair and square. I didn't run fast enough, and you can't win them all. But people couldn't accept that; they figured that if I won three gold medals at the Olympics, I should be able to win in a little old meet in Los Angeles. That's the kind of pressure I was under that season; besides that, I never did like running indoors anyway. I felt like an Amazon in an arena, performing for the blood-thirsty crowds. Nevertheless, no matter what city I was in, or what arena I was in, people turned out to see me run. So I felt I owed them the very best performance I could possibly give on that particular night—and I delivered it.

One of the most memorable things that ever happened to me happened that season. Coach Temple, my mother, and I were in Washington, D.C., for a meet and a banquet. An old friend of ours from Tennessee State, a guy who was a senior there when I was a freshman, he came over to see us and he said, "Don't run away, hang loose, I'll be back to you." He had always been active in politics in school, and we knew he had a big job in government someplace; what he did, we didn't know.

Well, he calls back and he talks to Coach Temple, and Coach Temple hangs up the phone and says, "Get dressed, we've got a big surprise coming." He said we were going to go to the White House and visit with President Kennedy.

"President Kennedy in the White House?" I asked. "What? . . . How? . . . Why?"

"Because he invited us over," Coach Temple said.

The first stop was the Executive Office Building across the street from the White House. There we met the Vice-President, Lyndon Johnson. He was nice at first, telling us he'd set up anything special we wanted to do while we were in Washington. Then, he put his feet up on the desk, and started babbling about something, and I got turned off on him. I felt his putting his feet up like that was disrespectful. But he won me back a little bit by giving me a lovely bottle of perfume on the way out.

Then we were escorted across the street to the White House. I was really impressed; it was beautiful; so many important-looking people were around, and the security guards were all over the place. All the way in, I was asking myself, "Does President Kennedy really want to see me?"

We got to the Oval Office, and his rocking chair was waiting for him. Secret Service men were all around the office, and they were real nice to us, talking about sports and the Olympics. After about five minutes, President Kennedy popped in. I liked him right away. He was nice—you could tell it by just looking at him. I didn't say anything at first; I mean, what do you say to the President of the United States . . . Hello? He sensed that we were nervous, and he took the lead. He started talking about sports real excited like, then he said, "What's everybody doing standing around? Let's all have a seat."

He walked over to the rocking chair, and he started talking to me about track. Then something really weird happened. He sat down—and he missed the chair. He fell smack on his behind. Everybody ran over to help him up, and we were mortified—I mean, how else do you react when you see the President of the United States miss his chair and fall on his behind? The Secret Service men picked him up, and he was laughing. In fact, he laughed so hard that he got us all to laughing.

Then he got into his chair, and he said to me, "It's not every day I get to meet an Olympic cham-

pion, just like it's not every day that you get to
meet a President." The thing I suspected about
President Kennedy was that he read the sports
pages of newspapers. He asked me if I liked all of
the nicknames I was picking up in the press, and
then he named them: "The Black Gazelle,"
"Mosquito," and so on. I told him no, and I told
him I thought the gazelle was a beautiful animal
and the Italian people, who gave me that
nickname, did so as an honor. Then he said, "We
got a phone call from that friend of yours from
Tennessee State, telling us you were in town.
When I found out, I said, 'Well . . . get her over
here.' It's really an honor to meet you and tell you
what a magnificent runner you are."

President Kennedy and I chatted for about
thirty-five minutes, and then he talked some with
my mother and Coach Temple. He gave me an
autographed picture to take with me, and he personally walked us out. I really liked him. So much
so, that in later years I went to work for his brothers Bobby and Teddy at a physical fitness camp in
Boston. The last thing President Kennedy said to
me on the way out that day was, "Wilma, I think
it's incredible that you ran all of those races over
there . . . and you won them all. You were undefeated."

After that trip to Washington, I started thinking to myself, "What's left? Where do I go from
here?" I thought some about going back to the
Olympics in 1964. Then I thought, "Look, you already won three gold medals. You go back in
1964, you had better win three more, or even

four, or else you're a failure. You lose in 1964, that's what people will remember—the loss, not the three golds in 1960."

So I started giving some thought to retiring, knowing full well that I couldn't run forever. But I wanted to make the decision myself, the decision on when to step down. I didn't want somebody else making it for me by beating me. So I started doing a lot of thinking about myself, the future, everything, and came to the conclusion that I wanted to go out on top, even if it meant going out a little earlier than I should have. Better go out early and on top, I figured, than too late and beaten. I spoke with Coach Temple about it, told him how I felt, and he agreed with me.

He said, "To go back to the Olympics in 1964, and lose will diminish everything you've already accomplished." I agreed wholeheartedly.

Meanwhile, Robert and I were back together. I knew I loved him and he loved me. Yolanda was growing up; she was still with my mother, and I felt it was time for me to take over that role, too. So I made a decision. I said to myself, "Go out running well, then end it. But don't end it until you're running well; if you're running poorly stay with it until you're back to where you belong, then leave. Give them something positive to remember you by."

Coach Temple was always asking me if I wanted to go here or there, to compete in this meet or that. One day, he said, "Rudolph, you up to competing against the Russians?"

"Why not?" I said.

"There's this dual meet with the Soviet Union coming up at Stanford University in California. You want me to enter you in it?"

"Yes," I said, "that's a good one." Then I started working seriously, thinking that this might be the right meet in which to end my career. I was running near peak and needed only to win a couple to go out in style. Coach Temple worked me hard; he put me five, six yards behind everybody else and made me catch up. He was still a little sore at me anyway, because I had told him that I was seriously considering marrying Robert, and I don't think he liked Robert, or else maybe he was a little jealous of Robert because Robert was taking me away from him. Anyway, he worked my tail off before that meet with the Russians. If I was going to go out in top form, he was going to make sure that there was no doubt in my mind.

I went out to Palo Alto and read all about the Russian runners in the newspapers. They were this, they were that. Fine. Comes the 100, and I win it easily. I was very satisfied with myself after that race. Coach Temple also had me entered in the relay, and in this event the Russian girls were very good. They were better relay runners, for some reason, than they were sprinters. Anyway, I've got the anchor leg, and I get the baton. This Russian girl is about forty yards ahead of me. I give chase, I start picking up speed, and I start closing on her. She's looking at me out of the corner of her eye, and the look is like, "What is this, I can't believe she's closing so fast." Well, I caught her, passed her, and won the race. That was it. I knew it. The crowd in the stadium was on its feet, giving me a standing ovation, and I knew what time it was. Time to retire, with a sweet taste.

After the meet, I was under the stands signing autographs for about an hour. Then I went over to this little bench, and I started untying my track shoes. This one little boy had been hanging around the whole time, hoping to get an autograph. But the way things are in autograph crowds, the little kids always get shoved out of the way. So this little boy comes over to me, with a pencil and a little piece of paper in his hand, and he says, so shyly, "Miss Rudolph . . . can I please have your autograph?" I looked at him, and I smiled, and I said to him, "Son . . . I'll do better than that." I had a ball-point pen on me, and took off my shoes and I signed my name to both of them. Then I handed them to the little boy.

He couldn't believe it; he kept saying, "Really? Really? You're giving me your track shoes?" I nodded and smiled, and he ran away, saying, "Thank you, thank you, thank you," all the way. So that's the way my track career officially ended.

I didn't hang up my spikes. I gave them away.

## 13

## Retirement

After retiring from track, I made a couple final goodwill trips, one to French West Africa for the United States government and another to Japan for the Baptist Christian Athletes group. Billy Graham, the evangelist, made that trip with us. After I came home from Japan, I decided to return to Clarksville for a while and decide what to do with the rest of my life.

Usually when I returned home from someplace, one of the first people I would call would be Coach Gray, my very first coach. Sometimes, I'd stop by the Burt High School and surprise him, just walk right into his classroom and say something silly, like "Boo." A couple times, I even snuck up behind him and put my hands over his eyes and dared him to guess who it was. Coach Gray and I had our moments years before, but now we were real good friends.

So when I returned to Clarksville from Japan, I was home for maybe an hour, and I called the school and asked if Coach Gray was in that day. I was told no, he wasn't. Now that was strange because he never took sick days off from school, that's just the way he was. So I just decided to drive over to his house later and see what was the matter with him.

I finished unpacking, and was just resting on my mother's bed when Robert walked in. He had a distorted look on his face, like something was wrong. He said, "Coach Gray ... he's just been killed in an automobile accident." I refused to believe it. I wouldn't believe it. I rushed over to the school in a daze.

When I got there, I ran right into the room of the music teacher, Mrs. Mildred Jones, knowing that she was a good friend of Coach Gray's. When she saw me, the look on her face changed, and I knew then that the news was true. She sat me down and we talked for a long while, and I told her that I had another trip to make to the Orient, and that I just couldn't take it because this was too shattering. She told me to go, that Coach Gray would have wanted me to go—after all, he started me off on this life. So I left behind a letter to be read at his funeral, and never went to the services. They would have been too much for me. I always preferred to think in terms of Coach Gray moving away, just off to another town and another job. At the time, I wanted to remember him for the good times and forget that he was dead.

So I left for the Orient on my last big trip and stayed there for two months. It revived my spirits, and when I got back to Clarksville the people at the high school were waiting for me. They offered me Coach Gray's job as the girls' track coach, and

I accepted it. I was to start in September, and I would also be teaching second-grade classes in the elementary school I had attended as a child.

But before that school year started, something good happened. Robert and I got married. It was an unusual wedding, to say the least. We talked about which church in Clarksville to hold the ceremony in, and there wasn't one in town big enough. So we finally hit on an unusual idea—an outdoor wedding, right on this big, open field, not far from where my mother lived in the projects. We went to a lady named Marie Vance in town— she was the florist, and she agreed to plan the whole thing. When she got through with it, the open field looked something like a church—it had an altar, flowers, chairs for all of the guests, and she even had the whole thing roped off. All of the flowers were in pale blue. Two of my sisters were in the wedding party, Robert's sister was in it, and the flower girl was our little daughter, Yolanda. Everybody in the projects, it seemed, turned out for the wedding. So did one of Robert's old girl friends. She apparently found out that he was getting married, and she flew down from Indiana, or Chicago, or someplace. She had no place to stay, but when she invited herself to the wedding, we told her don't worry, that she could stay with my grandmother. So what happens? She winds up crying during the whole ceremony, and *Jet* magazine has a photographer there, and he takes her picture with the tears rolling down her face. In the next issue of *Jet* magazine, the picture is in there with a caption that says, "Who was this woman crying

156

at Wilma Rudolph's wedding?" I was furious when I saw it, but forgot all about it in a couple hours.

Robert was real nervous during the wedding, so much so that he never noticed that the shirt to his tuxedo was missing some buttons. We had a reception that afternoon, right after the wedding, at my mom's house; then we had another reception at the big American Legion hall in town. Everybody in town, it seemed, came by at one time or another. The only person we didn't see that day was Coach Temple, and that really hurt. He apparently did not approve of my marrying Robert, or else he felt that Robert was taking me from him, or something. Anyway, he did not show up for the wedding. He refused to accept the marriage at the time, and for a long time after. He finally broke down, and he and Robert became friends.

We didn't have a honeymoon. Instead, we went to a family reunion of Robert's family, out in the country, and I had a chance to meet all of his relatives that I hadn't met yet. The reason we didn't have a honeymoon was because we simply couldn't afford one. We didn't have the money to take off anywhere. Robert was getting ready to enroll at Tennessee State himself, and I hadn't even begun my new teaching and coaching job yet. So we passed it up, saying we had seen so much of the world anyway, where else was there to go?

In September, I started teaching the second grade. I loved it. I was a typical teacher, taken up with the kids. I had an influence over them that is evident to this day; I see them today, as college sophomores, and they stop me and they start talking about the second grade and the good times they had.

During that school year, I became pregnant again. I was happy about that, but not exactly happy about the whole situation I was in. For one thing, as much as I loved teaching, I wasn't making any money at it, and I was supporting my family—not Robert—because he was in school. For another, I was back working with the same teachers I had had in school, and under the same principal. My idea of teaching was to bring new ideas into the classroom; after all, that's what I went to college for, to learn new ideas and methods. But they wanted to stay the same, no change, and they resisted everything I tried to do. I was frustrated by that. But I stayed with it until the very end of the school year; on May 19, 1964, my second daughter was born; we named her Djuana.

I watched the 1964 Olympics in bed, with my new baby. I had no feeling about not being in it. I had a new life now, and I was trying desperately to make it work. I was up and around again to start teaching that fall, but in the middle of that school year, I got pregnant again. That August, my first son was born; we named him Robert, Jr. When Robert walked into the hospital that day and was told he had a son, his reaction was, "Hey, I finally got a dude." So little Robert has been called "Dude" ever since, for obvious reasons. But just before the birth of Robert, during that long, hot summer pregnancy, I made a decision. I decided that I didn't want to stay in Tennessee any longer. I wasn't making any money, and I wasn't making any progress as a teacher. I did have a job offer to become director of a community center in Evansville, Indiana, and I took it. So to Indiana we all went.

The job itself was not all that bad, but I realized right away that it was not exactly what I wanted. So I had to start shopping around again. One day, I sat down at a typewriter and finger-pecked a letter to a woman I had met named Berdetta Washington, who was a leader in the Job Corps. I told her I would like to get involved in the Job Corps program and asked her for a job. I received a letter back from a man named Frank Bispham; he lived in Boston, and he was the personnel man for the Job Corps. He sent for me, and I went up to see him for an interview. He offered me a job at a Job Corps center in Poland Springs, Maine; the job was to run the girls' physical education program there—everything from conducting calisthenics to writing the curriculum. So we packed the family again and moved from Evansville to Maine. The center in Maine was a converted resort; the job was all right, and we stayed there for almost a year.

By now it was 1967. I received a letter one day from Hubert Humphrey, who was then Vice-President of the United States; the letter invited me to work for him as a member of what was called Operation Champ. The object of this program was to take star athletes into the sixteen largest city ghetto areas to give the kids some sports training. Ralph Boston and I were involved in track, Donna Deverona was hired to conduct swimming, Ollie Matson handled football, and some players from the Baltimore Bullets handled basketball. We went to Detroit, Cleveland, Chicago, Washington, Baltimore—every big city where there was a black ghetto—and taught our specialty sports to the kids.

Now, at the time, the black ghettos in big cities were going up in flames and in riots, and I guess we were all hired to help calm things down. But after working in such places, you came away with mixed feelings, or at least the feeling that you shouldn't sit in judgment of anybody. No, it's not necessarily right to burn and riot in ghettos, but on the other hand it's certainly not right for people to have to live under oppressed conditions. I saw those conditions myself, and I felt I could understand better than the average person why the people who lived in those places exploded the way they did. I grew up in a small, segregated Southern town, but the oppression there was nothing compared to the oppression I saw in the big city black ghettos.

When that assignment ended, I asked the Job Corps to transfer me out of Maine to someplace closer to Tennessee. I was sent to St. Louis. The Job Corps center there was located right in the middle of the black ghetto area, and I didn't stay there long. I felt that I had just gone through that sort of thing, and I wanted a change. I left St. Louis when my sister Charlene took ill in Detroit, and I went to live with her and to take care of her. I also took a teaching job at Pelham Junior High in Detroit; it was located right on 12th Street, the street where the famous Detroit riot had broken out. The kids there were terrific, all they needed were outlets, and I gave them one through track. They loved it, and I had a ball. I stayed there for a year and a half, then left because I felt I wanted more out of life for myself and my family. Eight years had gone by since I won the three gold medals in the Olympics, and I still hadn't found the fulfillment outside of track that I had found in it.

I left Detroit on the night Dr. Martin Luther King was killed. Earlier that day, my favorite aunt had died in Clarksville. I flew into Nashville that night and went with my children to the bus station to get back to Clarksville. There was incredible tension on the airplane, because everybody knew that something terrible had happened, a great American black leader had been assassinated in Tennessee, and yet nobody knew what to say about it. So nobody mentioned it, and the tension grew.

Inside the bus station, I was standing with my children, waiting to board the bus to Clarksville, and this white fellow came by and spit at my children. I saw red. I was ready to fight him on the spot. A black man who had been sitting there, watching the whole thing, called the police. When the police came, they arrested the white man and took him away. That topped off a very bad day. When I finally did get back to Clarksville, my family was in mourning over the death of my

161

aunt, and the rest of the black people were in mourning over the loss of Dr. King. I think that night was the absolute low point of my life, mentally. I became very depressed after that and couldn't seem to snap out of it.

One day, I had a long talk with Bill Russell, my friend from the 1956 Olympics who was now a big star with the Boston Celtics. I told him that I was really depressed, that nothing in my life had seemed to go right since 1960 and the Olympics. I asked him what should I do?

He said, "Try something completely different, a change of scenery. Try California. If you don't like it, you can always come back. But try it; you might like it."

So I said to myself, "Why not?" I went to Los Angeles by myself and lived there alone for a while, and then my family joined me. My first job there was working in the poverty area for the Watts Community Action Committee. I enjoyed the work, but the money wasn't there, either, and I found myself right back where I started. How can you support a family on peanuts? My mental state went back to depression again. I really didn't know what I was going to do, or where I was going.

One day, out of the clear blue sky, I got an invitation from this millionaire owner of an Italian newspaper to come to visit Italy. He said the Italian people all remembered me from 1960 and that I could visit the country again, and everything would be free. I jumped at the chance. I got there just as they were shooting a movie called, *The*

*Games*, which was about the Olympics. Rafer Johnson and Ryan O'Neal were both in the movie, and we all teamed up to go to operas in Rome and things like that when they weren't shooting. Coincidentally, much of the location shots were done in what remained of the Olympic stadium and village from 1960. It was like returning to the past, but what I really wanted out of that trip was some peace of mind. I knew that, since 1960, I had been a good wife and mother, but I was besieged with money problems; people were always expecting me to be a star, but I wasn't making the money to live like one. I felt exploited both as a woman and as a black person, and this bothered me very much, too.

Then I went and caught a cold. I was confined to bed, and one night while I was sleeping this young woman appears out of nowhere in my room. I thought I was dreaming at first, so I turned on the light. She was a pretty young girl, and she started asking me all of these questions. She said she was a reporter for the newspaper that was paying for my trip. I told her, "Look, I've got a cold, I'm confined to bed, this is the middle of the night and you're invading my privacy, and I'm not supposed to give interviews until it's cleared first." So she left.

The next day, in this newspaper—a communist newspaper, I find out—there is a big story that I'm being held prisoner, and that I'm not allowed to talk with anyone, that I don't have a job, and I'm living in poverty. I couldn't believe it. So I called a press conference and said, "Look, I've got a cold, the woman appears out of the blue sky in the middle of the night, asking questions. Who wouldn't be hostile under those circumstances? The story is true insofar as the job part of it is concerned, but the rest is false." What I didn't know at the time was that this Italian newspaper publisher was exploiting me, too. He wanted me to speak out against America and against capitalism and maybe even turn me into a communist as well. I told the press conference that I just hadn't found the work I was looking for in America, and that I had nothing against America per se. As soon as I shook the cold, I left Italy, and I haven't heard from the millionaire newspaper publisher since.

I went back to California and took a job at UCLA, as an administrator in the Afro-American Studies program. But I started getting the same old feedback—she was good in track, okay. Now, what else can she do? It was as if they were holding my track success against me. So I started job-hunting again and wound up landing one working for Mayor Daley's Youth Foundation program in Chicago. But that didn't last long, either. There was one administrator there who just wanted to use me—"There's Wilma Rudolph, she works for us now." But he wouldn't let me do anything. He told me when he hired me, "You sign on for this figure and after you're here for a month, you'll be raised automatically to this figure." Well, the raise never came, and he never mentioned a thing about it again.

I felt used and betrayed and exploited right

there. He would do things like reject my requisitions for equipment. I would tell him, "How can I run a program without any equipment?" So I took it upon myself to go get the equipment, anyway, and sign it all to the Mayor Daley Youth Foundation. He and I finally had a big fight over that, and I resigned.

Then I went to Charleston, West Virginia, where some people were trying to raise a million and a half dollars for a Track and Field Hall of Fame. I worked there as a fund-raiser, and I helped them meet their figure. I felt very deeply about having a track Hall of Fame, anyway. I was finally doing something that I believed in. I feel track is the backbone of sports in America; it's the one sport where American athletes get worldwide attention. Nobody in Europe knows American football players or baseball players, but they know the tracks stars.

When the million and a half was finally in, I left West Virginia. I was in debt again, my husband Robert was very ill, and I decided there was no place to go but back home.

Back in 1960, right after the Olympics, I used to silently wonder to myself, "Where will all of this end?" Here it is, over a decade and a half later, and I'm right back where it started, in Clarksville, Tennessee. Still, I'm proud of what I did. No matter what, I was the first American woman to win three Olympic gold medals. I was the first of twenty-two kids in my family to go to college. I was the only woman in history to pack Madison Square Garden in New York, the Forum in Los Angeles, and a lot of other places for track meets. People came to see me run. But the promoters made all of the money, not me. I was strictly an amateur, in more ways than one.

# 14

## Today

Today. Today I sometimes think about people like Alice Coachman and Mildred McDaniels. Not many people in America today know much about Alice Coachman and Mildred McDaniels, and that's why I think about them. They were black women track stars. Whatever became of them, I don't really know. But you won't find too much about them in libraries, and you won't see them on television shows, or hear them on the radio. Alice Coachman was a sprinter, and she goes way back; she was the first black woman ever to represent the United States in the Olympic Games. Mildred McDaniel doesn't go back as far, only to 1956 when she was the first black woman to win a gold medal for the United States in the Olympics. She was a high-jumper for Tuskegee Institute. Then, of course, there was Mae Faggs, who was black and who competed three times for the United States in the Olympics. You don't read or hear too much about her, either.

The fact of the matter is that black women athletes are on the bottom rung of the ladder in American sports. Most of them are involved in track and field because that's the only sports still really open to them. How many black women golfers are there, or how many black women tennis players? When their track careers are over, no matter what they've accomplished in the Olympics, there is no place for them to go. They wind up drifting back to where they began, and nobody ever hears from them again.

Sure, the situation should be changed, but who is going to tell the company presidents and the television executives and the advertising agencies to start making room for black women athletes? Who is going to invest a couple of million dollars for professional women's track, which is a logical place for black women athletes to go after their Olympic careers are over? Women's pro track in America has been a joke, because nobody has any money. They asked me a couple of times if I could get back into running shape and make a comeback in one of the pro circuits, and I asked, "How much will you pay me?" The answer was, "No money, just expenses." Baloney.

The traveling pro track circuits have been a failure because there is no money behind them, and because they insist on taking the circuit on the road instead of putting stationary teams in major cities. The way it has been, the same people run against each other every night in a different city. People won't pay to see that. But put teams in major cities, just like the other pro sports do, and maybe there would be a chance. But I don't see anything happening in that area, either, that would enable black women athletes to keep up their specialties and make some money, too.

So you're a black woman athlete from the South, and the doors to commercial success are pretty much closed to you, and people say, "Well, why don't you get involved in the women's lib movement and try to change things?" The answer is because the women's lib movement is not exactly relevant to my problems. The women's liberation movement is going around the country encouraging women to get out and get jobs. Black women have always worked, for many, many years now, because they had to, not because they wanted to acquire new identities. Black women worked to feed their families because so little was open to black men.

I know black women in Tennessee who have worked all of their lives, from the time they were twelve years old to the day they died. These women don't listen to the women's liberation rhetoric because they know that it's nothing but a bunch of white women who had certain life-styles and who want to change those life-styles. They say things like they don't want men opening doors for them anymore, and they don't want men lighting their cigarettes for them anymore. Big deal. Black women have been opening doors for themselves and lighting their own cigarettes for a couple centuries in this country. Black women don't quibble about things that are not important.

In my home town of Clarksville, for example, I would say that 95 percent of all the black women work at regular jobs, and they have been doing so all of their adult lives. That does not include coming home and raising the family. Black women have never known the luxury of spending their afternoons at PTA meetings, or going to League of Women Voters meetings, or even coming home and finding bouquets of roses waiting for them. They work because their husbands can't make enough money at their jobs to keep everything going. It's a fact of life,. They don't go to work to find fulfillment, or adventure, or glamour and romance, like so many white women think they are doing. Black women work out of necessity.

My own fulfillment today comes from my family, and I have no second thoughts about it. If I had it to do all over again, I would have done it the very same way. I never knew where the running career would end up, but I did know that nothing is forever and there would be a time when I had to stop running and go on to something else. I've never had any ambitions to coach track and field on the Olympic level, say, but I'm not discounting that possibility in future years. The reason I can't coach right now is because I'm still too close to it, even though sixteen years have passed since my own Olympic success. I get too excited, too involved, and I still have the runner's mentality, instead of a coach's mentality.

I see young girls at Tennessee State like Sandra Cheeseborough and Kathy MacMillion and Brenda Morehead, and I get excited for them. Both of them are very young and they are working under Coach Temple, and I know they're going to be stars some day. I go over to the campus every so often and watch the girls work out, and I give them a tip or two now and then. If they ask me, "What's going to happen to me if I become a successful runner," I'm honest with them about that, too.

My oldest daughter, Yolanda, who is eighteen now, is running at Tennessee State for Coach Temple. She's a freshman there, and I'm fully aware of the pressure she is under because of my past accomplishments at the same school. Right now, she is just an average runner, learning a lot. She's not fantastic, not flashy, and not especially fast. But she loves it. For one thing, the difference between me and her is size; I was much taller as an eighteen-year-old college freshman than she is. Second, you don't inherit speed. I never once pushed her into track and field, or anything, but she came to me a couple of years ago and said she was interested in becoming a runner herself. I let it ride for a whole year, until she was begging me for permission to go to Tennessee State and run. I finally said yes, then explained to her what is was going to be like being Wilma Rudolph's daughter there. "Don't try to live up to anything," I told her, "Be yourself."

My second daughter, Djuana, actually has a better chance of becoming a class runner than Yolanda has. Djuana is only twelve, but she is built like me, tall and skinny, and she's almost as fast as Yolanda right now. But she shows no interest in running whatsoever. She tried it a couple of times, and I was impressed with what I saw in her, but she came back and said, "Mom, I don't really like this because I get too tired and the whole thing is just too much work for me." I'm hoping that as she grows up she might show an interest, but if she doesn't, that's okay, too. She has her own life to live.

My two sons are still young, but both of them love football. One of them may turn out to be the next generation's O. J. Simpson, but we're just going to have to wait and see about that. Robert Jr. has already dislocated one shoulder in junior league football, and I don't know if it's going to be wise for him to keep playing the game if he keeps getting hurt. I don't want him seriously injured.

The future? I really don't know what it holds. I've settled with my family into a nice house in a suburb of Clarksville and plan to stay there. I can tell you this, though, whatever the future holds, I'll be ready for it, for I've learned a family's a powerful thing.

## Other SIGNET Books of Interest

## Other SIGNET Books of Interest